Nuts for Future Historians to Crack

Various

Contents

INTRODUCTION. 7

TO THE PUBLIC. 18

TO GENERAL JOSEPH REED. 22

NUTS FOR FUTURE HISTORIANS TO CRACK

BY

Various

NUTS FOR   Future Historians to Crack. COLLECTED BY

HORACE W. SMITH.

CONTAINING THE

CADWALADER PAMPHLET, VALLEY FORGE LETTERS

etc., etc., etc.

PHILADELPHIA:

HORACE W. SMITH, 20 SOUTH SIXTH STREET.

1856.

INTRODUCTION.

For some years I had been engaged in collecting material for a life of my great grandfather, the Rev. William Smith, D. D., Provost of the University of Pennsylvania, and in doing so, I read all the Bibliographical and

Historical works which I thought could in any way make mention of him. In no case did I find anything said against his character as a man, until I read Wm. B. Reed's Life of his grandfather, Gen. Joseph Reed. His remarks were uncalled for and ***ungentlemanly***; what they were, ***amount to nothing***, as they were ***untrue***; and therefore not worth repeating. My first idea was to speak of Gen. Joseph Reed in the same manner, though with more truth; but finding the truth had been suppressed, and that to publish all I could wish in regard to Reed, would take up too much room in my work, and be departing from my original design, I therefore, concluded to publish all the historical facts in regard to Reed in a small volume by itself, and to publish such an edition, that it could not be bought up and destroyed.

I have taken the liberty of using the following extracts from an article published in the Fireside Visitor--by J. M. Church. Whom it was written by I do not know, but the writer evidently understood his subject.

            *   *   *   *   *

"When it was announced that Mr. Irving was about to present to the public a life of Washington, we hailed the information with feelings of delight, not unmingled with gratitude, that the illustrious author of 'Columbus,' the Sketch Book, and Knickerbocker should make the crowning work of his life and literary labors, the history of the greatest and purest of patriots, so dear to the hearts of all his countrymen, and one who, the more time and investigation develop and explain his motives and actions, the greater and nobler he appears. Our expectations were great when we contemplated the vast field that time had laid open to the historian; and though Marshall and Sparks had left but little to do, we felt there was still enough to make Mr. Irving's the greatest history of that greatest of men.

On the appearances of the first volume, a number of errors were noticed by the press, which were subsequently corrected. The most important one, that in relation to Major Stobo, we are glad to see fully explained and corrected in a note at the end of the second volume. In the early part of the second volume, however, a far graver error occurs, we mean Mr. Irving's estimate of the conduct and character of Gen. Reed, and is it mainly the object of this communication to set that matter in its true light.

Who can read without emotion of the trials and difficulties that beset Washington throughout the whole of his career? A Congress so corrupt, that Livingston writes, 'I am so discouraged by our public mismanagement, and the additional load of business thrown upon me by the villainy of those who pursue nothing but accumulating fortunes, to the ruin of their country, that I almost sink under it.' False friends and traitors intrigue against him--even Gen. Reed, the very man Mr. Irving so delighted to honor, and an inmate of his household, writes a letter to Gen. Lee, the aspiring rival of Washington, reflecting, with harsh severity, on the conduct and character of his commander and benefactor. Lee's answer fell into the hands of Washington, and was read by him during the absence of Reed, who made no attempt at an explanation until Lee was taken prisoner. He then endeavored to explain the delay, by saying that he had been in the meantime endeavoring to get possession of his letter, in order that he might show to Washington that it contained nothing to call forth the violent answer of Gen. Lee, and, 'In the meantime,' writes Reed, 'I most solemnly assure you, that you would see in it nothing inconsistent with that respect and affection which I have, and ever shall bear to your person and character.' Who can read this without being shocked at the falsehood of the man!

It was, indeed, fortunate for Reed, that Washington never saw that letter. But how could Mr. Irving quote a portion of so important a document, while he suppressed the material part? Indeed, we are tempted to believe that some other hand had supervised those pages, before they were presented to the public.

We conceive it to be the duty of an impartial historian to collect facts, and present them to his readers, and he is guilty of falsifying history who suppresses them. His readers have the same right to *all* the evidence that bears upon important occurrence that he has, and though the author may give his views and conclusions, the reader is not of necessity compelled to agree with him. We for one, must beg leave to differ from Mr. Irving in his estimate of Reed's character, and we doubt not that every one reading his letter will sustain us in our opinion, that his conduct was false and treacherous in the extreme.

In order properly to appreciate the baseness of Reed's conduct, it is necessary to consider the circumstances under which it occurred. It was immediately after Washington had experienced the most trying reverses. Fort Washington had just been captured; over two thousand men had been taken prisoners, and his own eyes had beheld his men, partners of his toil, bayoneted and cut down while they begged for quarter. The Jerseys were overrun, and Philadelphia threatened by the enemy. Add to this, the accounts he received from Congress of the state of affairs at home, and it wanted but the discovery of such treachery to crush a spirit less mighty than his.

It appears strange that Mr. Irving should form such an undue estimate of Reed's character, nor can we believe him to be ignorant of what was his real position and standing among his brother officers. As early as 1776, when Reed contemplated resigning his commission as Adjutant General, the announcement was hailed with pleasure, for Reed had few friends. Col. Trumbull, writing to a member of Congress on the subject, says, "I heard Jos. Reed had sent his resignation some time ago; in the name of common sense, why is it not accepted? That man's want of abilities in his office had introduced the greatest disorders and want of discipline into the army; it ought to originate from that office. Then he had done more to raise and keep up a jealousy between the New England and other troops, than all the men in the army besides. Indeed, his *stinking pride*, as General George Clinton expresses it, has gone so far, that I expect every day to hear he is called to account by some officer or other; indeed, he is universally

hated and despised, and it is high time he was displaced." If Mr. Irving
has not seen that letter, we refer him to the New York Gazette, of December
the 9th, 1776, or to Mr. Peter Force's American Archives, if that work be
more accessible to him.

We have still another complaint of omission to make against Mr. Irving, and
we think it too important a point in the history of Gen. Reed to be
overlooked.

A few days previous to the battle of Trenton, when affairs were most
gloomy, and not a single star appeared to give the faintest glimmer of
hope, Reed appeared despondent: "He felt the game was up, and there was no
use of following the wretched remains of a broken army; he had a family,
and it was but right that he should look after their interests; besides,
the time had nearly expired during which they could avail themselves of the
pardon offered by Gen. Howe to all those who should go over to the enemy."
Such were the lamentations of Gen. Reed, until, in the agony of his fears,
he communicated them to Gen. Cadwalader. The feelings of that high-minded,
chivalrous soldier can hardly be imagined--his first impulse was to order
Reed under the arrest, but was deterred for fear of the effect the example
might have on the men. He, however remonstrated with him, and his arguments
appeared for the time to restore his composure. During the night previous
to the battle of Trenton, Reed lay concealed in Burlington, in anxious
expectation of the result of Washington's great master-stroke.

He had opposed the enterprise in his communications with Washington, by the
most discouraging representations, and now anxiously awaited the result.

His fears were worked up to the highest pitch; and the burthen of his
conversation was, how he should protect himself. He had with him a
companion in his weakness, and the determination they both came to was, to
go over to the enemy early in the morning. Before, however, they could

execute their intentions, the news arived of the victory of the Americans, the turning point in our country's fortunes, which gave hope to the people and courage to Gen. Reed.

A few years after these transactions, Reed was accused in the public newspapers of having meditated a desertion to the enemy. He replied in a pamphlet, in which he attempted to defend himself, and addressed it to Gen. Cadwalader, whom he conceived to be the author of the charges and between whom and himself there was some unfriendly feelings, arising out of pecuniary transactions between them. Cadwalader came out with a crushing[A] "Reply," in which though he denied having published the statements in the newspapers, he yet affirmed the truth of them, and brought such overwhelming *proofs* to sustain his charges, that the public lost all confidence in Reed, and failed to re-elect him to the office he had just held. It is not within the limits of an article like this to go through Gen. Cadwalader's pamphlet, suffice it to say, he was supported by Alexander Hamilton, Dickinson, Doct. Rush, Bradford, and numerous others. Among other things, it was proved that previous to the battle of Trenton, Reed had sent to Count Dunop, who commanded at Bordentown, to ask if he could have a *protection* for himself and *a friend*. The messenger narrowly escaped being hanged, through the intercession of a friend of Count Dunop. This is corroborated by an extract from the Diary of "Mrs. Margaret Morris."

Extract from a Journal kept by Margaret Morris, for the amusement and information of her sister Mitcah Martha Moore. Her residence at the time, was on the "bank" at Burlington, N. J., at the corner of Ellis Street.

*   *   *   *   *

"January 4th, 1777, we were told by a woman who lodged in the same room where General Reed and Colonel C---- took shelter, when the battle of Trenton dispersed the Americans, that they (Reed and C----) had laid awake all night consulting together about the best means of securing themselves, and that they came to the determination of setting off next day as soon as it was light to the British Camp, and joining them with all the men under their command. But when the morning came an express arrived with an account

that the Americans had gained a great victory. The English made to flee before the ragged American Regiments. This report put the rebel General and Colonel in high spirits, and they concluded to remain firm to the cause of America. They paid me a visit, and though in my heart I despised them--treated them civilly, and was on the point of telling them their conversation the preceding night had been conveyed to me on the wings of the wind, but on second thought gave it up--though perhaps the time may come when they may hear more about it."

There is still another page in the life of Gen. Reed that remains to be told, and that is the attempt alleged to have been made by Mrs. Ferguson to bribe him. All are familiar with his intensely patriotic reply, refusing *ten thousand pounds*, and the best office in the colonies, in his Majesty's gift. To be sure, Gov. Johnstone,[B] in a speech before Parliament, most emphatically denied having employed[C] Mrs. Ferguson to offer to Gen. Reed any bribe whatever, while at the same time he admits that *other* means besides persuasion were used. Does he allude to the pair of elegant pistols that Reed accepted after the attempt to bribe him, and with which he was charged in the public papers? But Mr. Irving has not yet approached this delicate subject, and to his able hands we leave it, fully conscious he will give it the attention so important a circumstance requires.

Should he fail, however, to do justice to Gen. Reed in this matter, he will pardon us if we again take the liberty of addressing him on the subject.

We have been careful in our strictures upon the character and conduct of Gen. Reed to assert nothing that unquestionable evidence does not sustain;

and if by our remarks we have lowered him from the undeserved eminence to which the injudicious zeal of interested parties has so industriously labored to elevate him, this result must rather be attributed to the weakness of the support, and the frailty of the statue, than to the vigor of the blows we have bestowed upon it.

The most we have done has been to remove the deceptive varnish, and the idol has fallen to pieces.

    T. S. P.

Proceedings of a General Court Martial of the line, held at Raritan in the State of New Jersey, for the trial of Major General Arnold, Published by order of Congress, Philadelphia.

Printed by Francis Bailey in Market Street, 1780.

Extract from the defence of General Arnold.

    *   *   *   *   *

"On this occasion I think I may be allowed to say, without vanity, that my conduct, from the earliest period of the war to the present time, has been steady and uniform. I have ever obeyed the calls of my country, and stepped forth in her defence, in every hour of danger, when many were deserting her cause, which appeared desperate. I have often bled in it; the marks that I bear, are sufficient evidence of my conduct. The impartial public will judge of my services, and whether the returns that I have met with are not tinctured with the basest ingratitude. Conscious of my own innocence, and the unworthy methods taken to injure me, I can with boldness say to my persecutors in general, ***and to the chief of them in particular***, that in the hour of ***danger*** when the affairs of America wore a ***gloomy aspect***, when our illustrious general was retreating through New Jersey, with a handful of men, I did not propose to my associates basely to quit the general, and sacrifice the cause of my country to my personal safety, by going over to the enemy and making my peace.

"I can say I never basked in the sunshine of my general's favour, and courted him to his face, when I was at the same time treating him with the greatest disrespect, and villifying his character when absent. *This is more than a ruling member of the Council of Pennsylvania can say,"* as it is *alleged and believed.*

The first edition of the Cadwalader Pamphlet was published in the year 1782, within the last twenty years all the copies, or nearly so, have been spirited away--where or by whom no one knows. They have been stolen from the public libraries and from the book cases of private individuals. In 1848 a second edition was issued. The publisher of this edition was threatened with prosecution, and although but six years have passed, it is now looked upon as a valuable curiosity. To the second edition was prefixed the following Introduction.

"A few years since a writer, over the signature of "Valley Forge," published in an evening paper of Philadelphia, called the "*Evening Journal*," and put forth certain statements connected with our revolutionary history, which caused a great excitement, and led to a challenge of an interview with the author, by the descendants of a person, whose character was considered as involved in doubt, as to his being a patriot of 1776. The party challenged failed to attend the proposed meeting, and this pamphlet will give a clue to the whole writings of "Valley Forge," and justify completely the course pursued by the editor of the "*Evening Journal*," who is not now of this world, and of course a matter immaterial perhaps to his friends and relatives.

NOTES.--"The allusion to the disrespectful treatment of the General refers in part, (I fancy) to the letter addressed by

General Charles Lee to Reed, which came to head quarters and was opened by Washington."--See Life of Joseph Reed.

"Joseph Reed at the time of the prosecution of Arnold was President of the Supreme Executive Council of Pennsylvania, and as is well known, took an active and prominent part against him."--See Spark's Life of Arnold, page 140.

The letter of Major Lennox and P. Dickinson refer to a person whose name is not mentioned, who was included in the application to Count Donop for a protection. There certainly must be in the possession of some of the descendants of revolutionary families, evidence to show who this person was: and it may yet be produced, to do justice to the memory of the men who figured in those times.

Trenton, December 26th, 1846.

The Valley Forge Letters were originally published in the Evening Journal, edited by Reuben Whitney, Esq., in the year 1842. I have given the printer the cuttings from that paper, so that the reader will get them in the exact condition in which they appeared, perhaps not in the same order.

A REPLY TO Genl. JOSEPH REED'S Remarks ON A LATE PUBLICATION IN THE INDEPENDENT GAZETTEER; WITH SOME OBSERVATIONS ON HIS

ADDRESS TO THE PEOPLE OF PENNSYLVANIA. By General John Cadwalader.

WITH THE LETTERS OF

Gen. George Washington, Gen. Alexander Hamilton, Major David Lennox, Dr. Benjamin Rush, Gen. P. Dickinson, Gen. Henry Laurens and others.

*   *   *

PHILADELPHIA:

PRINTED AND SOLD BY T. BRADFORD.

In Front Street, the fourth door below the Coffee-House.

1783.

TO THE PUBLIC.

When an appeal is made to the public by a person who has interested himself in the affairs of America from the beginning of the present revolution, he has a claim to their attention, with respect to transactions that reflect either upon his political conduct or principles as a patriot.

I wish, most sincerely, that all prejudices in favor or against General Reed or myself, may be laid aside on the present occasion, and that truth and justice may influence the determination of the public.

The world is now in possession of General Reed's address to me, relating to a conversation I had with him at Bristol, in the winter of 1776, and as it contains the grossest reflections upon my character, as a man of veracity and a patriot, it is incumbent on me to reply.

Mankind have been much the same, in every age, with respect to their conduct in political life. Their minds have been inflamed by the same passions, prejudices, and resentments, and parties have been supported by complaints and representations, which naturally grow into invective and personal abuse.

From these principles, General Reed has deduced those arguments and conclusions, which he vainly affects to think will justify him in asserting, that my conduct has been influenced by motives of hatred, resentment, and disappointed ambition. But when it shall appear, from the testimony I have inserted in the following sheets, that the conversation alluded to was spoken of by me in confidence, at a time when he asserts that all former personal dislike was removed, and that "we united in confidence and danger at the battle of Monmouth;" at a time, too, when he admits, that "no party or prejudices existed, (at least as to him,") the premises from which he has drawn his conclusions must be removed, and consequently his arguments fall with them.

If my bare affirmative against his negative was the only foundation on which the public were to found their judgment, our several characters, in the article of veracity, would be fairly weighed by candor, and a verdict given in favour of the preponderating scale. If, then, I had hazarded an assertion, without other (the most respectable) testimony to support it, the consciousness of my own integrity would have suppressed any fears with respect to the public opinion.

The many and hasty movements of my family during the present contest, have displaced several valuable papers relating to property as well as military affairs. I do not, however, despair of yet finding important ones relating to this matter, that may some time hence be published. But what need is there of more than I shall here adduce; since every prejudiced mind must feel (if not acknowledge) the testimony too respectable and powerful to admit of apology or reply. Testimony, too, obtained, (in many instances,) from persons to whom I am scarcely known,--persons residing in other States, who cannot be supposed to be the particular enemies of General Reed, or in any way connected with the politics of Pennsylvania.

Many other certificates, supporting and confirming those I shall here offer to the public are omitted, as it is thought they will swell the publication to an unnecessary size; and affidavits may, if required, be obtained to all the certificates which appear in this pamphlet.

        *   *   *   *   *

As the publication signed "Brutus," addressed to General Reed, containing certain queries, is referred to, it is thought necessary to reprint it.

To the Printer of the Independent Gazetteer.

SIR,--It is much to the honor of America, that in the present revolution, there have not been many instances of defection among officers of rank in the Continental army. In Oliver Cromwell's time, we frequently see a general fighting one day for the King, another for the Parliament; so unstable and wavering were the opinions of those republicans.

The corruption of the times is now become a universal complaint, and one would be almost tempted to believe, that the former days were better than these; that our forefathers were possessed of greater moral rectitude than the present generation, did not history and experience convince us of the contrary. There is, however, one great evil peculiar to this age--that of assuming the credit of being endowed with virtues to which we are perfect strangers. Cunning, address, and eloquence, have often misled the honest but too credulous multitude, and they have been taught to consider many a man as a patriot and a hero, whose real character was marked with nothing but deceit and treachery to his country. It is also amazing, that such men should meet with the highest success, and bear their blushing honors thick upon them, whilst modest merit and true patriotism could neither gain the suffrages of the people, nor the approbation of those who held the reins of government.

The reflections I am now making have, in a striking manner, been verified in this State. I should be extremely sorry to accuse without a just foundation, or to adduce a charge, were I not convinced that it is of the utmost importance that the public,--the people at large--should be enabled to form a right opinion of such men, who have been honoured, or may be honoured with their suffrages, and thereby exalted to places of the highest trust and confidence.

Impressed with this idea, and with a design to elucidate such characters, I shall take the liberty to propose to the public the following queries:

1. Was not General R----d, in December, 1776, (then A----t G----l of the Continental army,) sent by General Washington to the commanding officer at Bristol, with orders relative to a general attack intended to be made on the enemy's post at Trenton, and those below, on the 25th, at night?

2. Two or three days before the intended attack, did not General R----d say, in conversation with the said commanding officer at his quarters, that our affairs looked very desperate, and that we were only making a sacrifice of ourselves?

3. Did he not also say, that the time of General Howe's proclamation, offering pardon and protection to persons who should come in before the 1st of January, 1777, was nearly expired, and that Galloway, the Allens, and others, had gone over, and availed themselves of the pardon and protection offered by the said proclamation?

4. Did not he, General R----d, at the same time say, that he had a family, and ought to take care of them; and that he did not understand following the wretched remains of a broken army?

5. Did he not likewise say to the said commanding officer, that his brother, (then a colonel or lieutenant-colonel of

militia,) was at Burlington with his family, and that he had advised him to remain there, and if the enemy took possession of the town, to take a protection and swear allegiance?

It is well for America, that very few general officers have reasoned in this manner; if they had, General Howe would have made an easy conquest of the United States. And it is very obvious, that officers of high rank, with such sentiments, can have no just pretensions to patriotism or public virtue, and can by no means be worthy of any post of honour or place of trust, where the liberties and interest of the people are immediately concerned.

BRUTUS.

Philadelphia, September 3, 1782.

TO GENERAL JOSEPH REED.

In the first part of your late publication, which is no less an invective against me, than it is a defence of yourself, you have, with sufficient art, insisted on my remarkably contentious, factious,[D] and jealous spirit, which suffers no man, undisturbed, to enjoy his well-earned fame; a circumstance in my character you expected to derive considerable benefit from in the controversy between us. For this point being once gained, every suggestion, every article of charge against you, which has its foundation and support in me, would naturally be referred to those fierce and malignant passions you have so unsparingly bestowed on me, and no longer rest upon the general credit and reputation I trust I have acquired and maintained. But as I cannot, without injustice to myself, make this concession to you, I must declare my general tenor of conduct to have been far otherwise,--that in my private life I have been at peace and harmony with all mankind; and in my public, at enmity only with such public men as have disgraced their country by their vices or injured it by their crimes.

Wherein until the present, except in a single instance, have I drawn the public attention by attacks upon the character of any man? and that instance, an impostor, like yourself, who had got into a seat of honor. In this, it was virtue to become his accuser.

If you rely upon *your* instance, as affording a proof of my eagerness for controversy, it will not answer your purpose. I have not brought you to the public bar; for, whatever was the amount of your offences, I neither urged nor wished a public inquiry; another has brought you there, and I appear only as a witness against you, challenged and defied by yourself.

This being premised, I shall enter upon my subject, and reply to such parts of your pamphlet as respect me, and therefore specially concern me to notice.

Your remarks, you say, are with propriety addressed to me; because though not the actual author, it is to me you are really indebted for the insidious attempt on your reputation.

That the public may have the most authentic proofs of the manner in which I have been involved in this controversy, I think it necessary here to insert the original letters that passed in the course of our correspondence, last fall, on this subject.

SIR,--I have, for a long time, treated the anonymous abuse which disgraces our public papers with the contempt it deserves. But in Oswald's paper, of last Saturday, are a set of queries, signed Brutus, in which the author, not daring to make an open assertion, has insinuated, that in 1776 I meditated a desertion to the enemy. Though my soul rises with indignation at the infamous slander, I should treat it with scorn, if it did not seem to deserve some credit from a reference to you. Prejudiced, as I know you are, I should be sorry to suppose you capable of propagating such a sentiment, or decline the opportunity of doing justice to my character, and in some degree your own. And this for two reasons: first, the gross falsehood of the insinuation; and, secondly, to preserve a consistency in your own character, which must suffer from your placing such confidence in me, with respect to the military operations of that period, and permitting General Washington to do the same, after such a conversation as these queries suppose. I need make no apology, in this case, for requesting an immediate answer,--and am, sir,

Your obedient humble servant,
JOSEPH REED.

Market Street, Sept. 9, 1782.
Gen. Cadwalader.

SIR,--In answer to your letter, which I received last evening by Mr. Ingersoll, relating to queries published in Mr. Oswald's paper of last Saturday, signed Brutus, I can assure you, (as I did Mr. Ingersoll,) that I am not the author of that publication; nor have I published one single word, since I came from Maryland, relating to the politics of this state;

yet my character has, unprovoked, been traduced by you, or some of your friends. But, sir, I have repeatedly mentioned the substance of those queries to individuals immediately after the conversation alluded to happened; and since that time in many mixed companies. As charges of the same nature had some time since been made against you, to which you never made a reply, the world very justly concluded they were true; especially as the rank and character of the person who made the charge (at that time) merited your notice. From this circumstance, it occasioned an additional surprise, that you should, in this instance, undertake to investigate the matter, and declare in your letter to me, that the "insinuation" was "a gross falsehood." I therefore now assert, that in a conversation with you at the time and place mentioned in the above publication, signed Brutus, that you expressed the substance, and I think the very words, contained in the queries. If my character for veracity wanted credit with the world, one or two other gentlemen could be named, who, at nearly the same time, heard expressions from you, which created in them sentiments unfavourable to your character. You seem to insinuate that there is an inconsistency in my conduct, because I afterwards reposed a confidence in you, and because I permitted General Washington to do the same. It would have been very dangerous, at that critical period, to have exposed your weakness and timidity to the militia, as such an example might have been attended with the most fatal consequences to our cause. And as your conduct, upon this occasion, appeared to me to proceed from want of fortitude, and not the baser motives,--and as from the observations I made to you at the time, you seemed to resume more spirited sentiments in conversation, as well as from political motives, I continued to show an appearance of confidence, and concluded it best not to mention it to the General. The successes that soon followed gave a happy turn to our affairs, and thus, you, (with many others,) appeared to possess firmness in prosperity who had shown a want of it in times of imminent danger.

If your conduct in civil life had been such as could have been approved of, former transactions might have been buried in oblivion. But when I see a man endeavouring to injure the reputation of those, whose principles and conduct, from the beginning of the contest, have been uniformly exerted to obtain those ends intended by the revolution; and when he denies all merit to those who are not equally violent with himself, it is difficult to be silent.

I am, sir, your obedient servant,

Philadelphia, 10th Sept., 1782.   JOHN CADWALADER.

General Reed.

Philadelphia, Sept. 10, 1782.

SIR,--After waiting some time, and being just about to set off for Bucks, I received your letter of this morning, and am at a loss which to admire most, the depravity of your heart, or the weakness of your understanding. Your quoting General Arnold's testimony to vindicate your own falsehood is perfectly consistent. You shall hear further from me on my return from Bucks. In the mean time, I have made inquiry of Messrs. T. Smith and Shippen, whom you mentioned to Mr. Ingersoll as hearing from you sentiments similar to those in the queries, with a view of communicating them to me; which they never did, because they deny the least recollection of any such information; which must have been too striking to them, and interesting to me, to have passed unnoticed. Your talent for invention is also displayed on this occasion most probably.

Whatever you may suppose, several of my friends well know, that I have been anxious to trace some loose reports that I had heard, which your residence in Maryland, and the improbability of your saying such things, had induced me to neglect.

As to your insinuation of my writing against you in the newspapers, or its being done with my privity, it is equally groundless with all the rest. I have not wrote in the newspapers for a long time, nor at any time in my life respecting you.

I am, sir, your very humble servant,

General Cadwalader. JOSEPH REED.

To General Reed.

SIR,--I shall make no reply, *at this time*, to the expressions contained in your letter of the 10th inst.; but as you inform me that you are on the point of setting off for Bucks, I do not think it incumbent on me to remain here until you return, especially as I informed Mr. Ingersoll, that I intended leaving town as soon as the dust was laid, and wished you to take your measures as soon as possible, as I should make my arrangements accordingly. Some of my servants are gone, and I have every thing packed up; it will, therefore, be very inconvenient to detain my family, as you do not mention when you purpose returning. As you say I shall hear from you on your return from Bucks, I must inform you, that the post leaves this city for the Eastern Shore every Wednesday, at three o'clock; be pleased to direct to me, in Kent County, Maryland, to be left at Stewart's. You shall have my answer by the return of the post, or if necessary, I shall attend in person for further investigation.

I am, sir, your obedient servant,

Philadelphia, 12th Sept., 1782.   JOHN CADWALADER.

SIR,--Mr. Clymer delivered me your letter of the 12th instant. Your sudden departure from this city was indeed unexpected,--your declaration to Mr. Ingersoll not implying it to be so very soon;[E] and I should have supposed that my letter of the 10th, would have some weight to protract your journey. Before I received yours of the 10th, I had prepared a small publication, which the receipt of your letter did not influence me to alter or delay; as no signature could change the nature of things, and make falsehood truth, or truth falsehood. Having there declared the insinuation in Oswald's paper of the 7th instant to be false, I now apply the same epithet to your avowal of them; and am sorry, though not surprised, that your violence of temper should have occasioned such a deviation from the line of veracity so essential to the character of a gentleman.

I am already possessed of sundry authentic documents; a few days will complete them,--not to show my innocence,--the improbability of your charge, and inconsistency of your own conduct, making that unnecessary; but to show to what lengths a rancorous heart, puffed up by sudden and accidental wealth, can push a man of weak judgment and ungovernable passions.

I need not give you my address, though I think it incumbent on me to assure you, that if by investigation you mean a personal interview, I will endeavour to make it as convenient as possible, and will shorten the distance between us.

I am, sir, your obedient humble servant,

Philadelphia, 23d Sept., 1782.   JOSEPH REED.

General Cadwalader.

Maryland, 30th September, 1782.

SIR,--I received yours of the 23d inst. by the post. From the style of your first letter, (9th Sept.) in which you required an "immediate answer," I fully expected an immediate interview. As you declined the interview I proposed through Mr. Ingersoll, and left town the next morning, without saying when you proposed returning, and having determined not to "alter or delay" the "small publication," which you "had prepared before the receipt of my first letter,"--I am at a loss to know what could have occasioned your surprise at my departure, before your return from Bucks. After having promised to the public the most satisfactory proofs, that no such conversation as alluded to in the queries ever passed, it was reasonable to allow you some time to prepare your "authentic document." Your last letter (23d Sept) informs that they were not *then* completed. And could you reasonably expect that I should have remained in town till this is completed? or could you suppose I would suffer your publication, worked up, as it no doubt will be, with all the cunning and misrepresentation you are master of, to pass

unanswered? As you have protracted this affair by your
engagement to the public, I shall not put it in the power of
accident to deprive me of the opportunity of laying the
facts I am possessed of open to public view. The question will
then be, whether what I have avowed is true? My wealth,
judgment, or passions, can have no influence, either way, with
impartial men. My own character, the character of others
concerned, and all the circumstances combined, will determine
the judgment of the public. This business being ended, an
interview may reasonably be expected.

I am, sir, your humble servant,
Gen. Reed, Philadelphia.   JOHN CADWALADER.

Having for several years given over every expectation of seeing those
changes made in the constitution of Pennsylvania, which I have ever thought
necessary to secure that happiness and liberty intended by the revolution,
I retired, and have never since even expressed my sentiments concerning the
politics of this state, except among my particular friends. Your vexatious
administration hath furnished an example, to what a dangerous length the
authority of government may be carried under such a constitution.

The particular circumstances of my family made it necessary to spend a few
months in this city, last summer, without an intention of taking up my
residence here till the conclusion of the war; and though I never
interfered in politics here, except among my particulr friends, I was
attacked, in the public papers, by a party blindly devoted to you and your
measures; I made no reply, from a confidence that such intimations could
not injure me with those whose good opinion I regarded. But whether a
friend published the piece signed Brutus, in the mere spirit of
retaliation, or whether it was calculated for political purposes, at the
last election, let the author determine. The conversation, alluded to in

the queries, was known to many long before that period; among whom were some of your friends, in proof of which I offer Mr. Prior's certificate.[F]

Having mentioned the conversation *publicly*, those who heard it were certainly at liberty to make what use of it they saw proper.

Being entrusted with the command of the militia and a New England brigade, which lay at Bristol in December, 1776, I had permission from the Commander-in-chief to make an attack on the enemy, whenever I thought it could be done with success; I was prepared on the evening of the 22d December, to attempt the enemy's post, above the Black Horse, with seven hundred men; and about nine or ten o'clock, P. M., I received a letter from the general, requesting, if the enterprise was not too far advanced, to lay it aside, as he intended a general attack on the enemy's posts in a few days. From this circumstance, it appears, that the general gave me the information relating to the intended attack, the evening before you received his letter of the 23d December, in which the precise time was fixed. As he knew my intention to command the party myself, and therefore I might not be at Bristol the next day, this will account for his letter, of the 23d being directed to you. But here you mean to convey an idea that a preference in this communication was intended to you, though he had given me, in effect, the same information the evening before. This, too, you adduce as a proof of the general's "unbounded confidence in you," and you say you were sent by General Washington for the "express purpose of assisting me;" and "whatever my abilities were, that I had less experience of actual service than you had,--that you were received with cool civility, and very few marks of private attention;" though you acknowledge that I, at the same time, consulted you without reserve on our "military affairs." I will admit, that your opportunities of acquiring experience were greater than mine; and considering the extensive command I then had, (which was in number nearly equal to the force under the immediate command of General Washington,) I should have thought it no reflection on my abilities; nor would it have hurt my feelings, if an officer of superior abilities and rank had been sent to take the command,--or even an *inferior* officer to assist me. But whether your appointment was of the mere *motion* of the commander-in-chief, or at your instance, (for assisting me or *other purposes*,) may at least become a *question*.

That I received you "with cool civility, and very few marks of private attention," I do not remember; but to give what you mean to convey its full force, I will not hesitate to acknowledge it in its fullest extent; as you have granted, that I consulted "without reserve on our military affairs." In this instance, the world will do me justice, as it appears that I did not suffer personal dislike to interfere with public duty.

Though the world have little to do with the causes of private animosities, I shall think myself perfectly excusable, here to say a few words on this subject, as you have assigned causes for the interruption of our intimacy different from the true ones, and with a view of creating prejudices against me.

I acknowledge that such intimacy subsisted between us in early life, and you malignantly date its "dissolution" at the time of my sudden accession of fortune as owing thereto. If I were to admit, that you could properly date this breach from the moment you mention, I flatter myself, you would find it very difficult to persuade those who know me, to believe that to be the true cause. But this was really not the fact. The unworthy measures you took to evade the payment, (till compelled by a judgment of the court,) of Mr. Porter's order on you in favor of my brother and myself, which you had accepted, (to be paid out of a bond assigned by said Porter to you in trust,) was the true motive of that dissolution you complain of. If you turn to the records of the court, or review the correspondence with my brother on that subject, you must blush at such a subterfuge. From *that* time, and owing thereto, I avoided your company. I could here make the proper reflections, with respect to your veracity and integrity, but the world will do you justice.

The critical situation of our affairs, in the winter of 1776, is well known to every inhabitant of the United States; but those only who were at that time in the field, can have a true idea of the circumstances which often threatened the dissolution of the militia. My situation gave me better opportunities of knowing the feelings and temper of both officers and privates, than any other person; and the happy expedients used on several occasions, to prevent their going home in a body, are well known to many officers whom I then had the honour to command.

The first intimation we had of the capture of General Lee, was received by a flag which arrived at my quarters. To determine whether this was a misfortune, or an advantage to the cause of America, is at this time immaterial. It was then, however, generally thought a matter of great magnitude, in the British as well as in the American camp. The effect it had on our army is well remembered by those who were present, but particularly on the militia.

That men attached to a cause upon principle, should persevere in a prosperous situation of affairs, is not uncommon. We were at that time separated from our enemies only by a river, which we expected every day might be passable on the ice,--greatly inferior in number and discipline, and almost destitute of everything necessary even for defence. Add to this, a proclamation of General Howe, offering pardon and protection to those who should submit and swear allegiance before the first of January, 1777, and this time nearly expired. I say, under such circumstances, it would be wonderful indeed, if no officer of the army sunk under the apprehension of those dangers that threatened him. That there were more than *yourself*, I well know, whose expressions discovered a timidity unworthy an officer and a patriot, who, notwithstanding, from the well-timed and spirited remonstrances of their friends, were induced to assume a firmer tone of behaviour, and have since rendered their country considerable services.

Having fully stated the temper of men's minds at this alarming period, and the situation of public affairs, I shall now recite the conversation and circumstances relating thereto, which I have avowed in my letter to you of the 10th September, as having passed between us at Bristol.

I had occasion to speak with you a few days before the intended attack on the 26th December, 1776, and requested you to retire with me to a private room at my quarters; the business related to intelligence; a general conversation, however, soon took place, concerning the state of public affairs; and after running ever a number of topics,--in an agony of mind, and despair strongly expressed in your countenance and tone of voice, you spoke your apprehensions concerning the event of the contest,--that our affairs looked very desperate, and we were only making a sacrifice of ourselves; that the time of General Howe's offering pardon and protection to persons who should come in before the first of January, 1777, was nearly expired; and that Galloway, the Allens, and others, had gone over, and availed themselves of that pardon and protection, offered by the said proclamation; that you had a family, and ought to take care of them, and that you did not understand following the wretched remains (or remnants) of a broken army; that your brother (then a colonel or lieutenant-colonel of militia,--but you say of the five months' men, which is not material,) was then at Burlington, with his family; and that you had advised him to remain there, and if the enemy took possession of the town, to take a protection and swear allegiance; and in so doing he would be perfectly justifiable.

This was the substance, and I think nearly the very words; but that "you did not understand following the wretched remains (or remnants) of a broken army*," I perfectly remember to be the* very words *you expressed.*

That our situation was critical, and the dangers that threatened us great, were universally acknowledged; but I was astonished to hear such expressions from the Adjutant-General *of the army, as your conduct had been approved of by report; for your good behaviour was not personally known to me. Judging from appearances, and from all circumstances at the time, I imputed these sentiments* solely to timidity; and therefore, to rouse your feelings, and give new vigor to a mind weakened by fear, I recalled to your memory your former public professions and conduct, and endeavoured to paint, in the strongest colours, the fatal consequences, that would ensue from such an example, particularly to the militia; that if officers, (more especially one in your station,) discovered a want of firmness, we could not reasonably expect private soldiers to remain in the field; and added, that as I was commanding officer there, I should not pass over such expressions in future; appearing to be invigorated by these remonstrances, your subsequent conversation induced me to hope from you a more honourable resolution. The immediate turn in our affairs confirmed this hope. I had, besides, at the moment, a still stronger dissuasive. I foresaw that an "arrest," or discovery, on my part, would produce all the bad effects naturally to be apprehended from actual desertion; I mean with respect to the discouragement which such an example would have caused in the army, but particularly in the militia; and especially, as at that time the militia were assembling at Philadelphia, under General Putnam, from every part of the country, influenced by the example of the city troops, as well as by a sense of danger and duty. If, then, the city militia had disbanded, no person can hesitate to determine what would have been the fate of those from the country.

The reasons of my concealing it from the General were, that nothing but an arrest, on his part, could have prevented the execution of this plan of desertion, and the bad consequences ensuing from it, the betraying of secrets; and such arrest would have wrought the *other* ill consequences I have spoken of. In this dilemma, I used a discretion which I considered most advantageous to my country; and trusted to my hopes, that so important an event, as your defection, would not happen, and thus avoid the *immediate* and *certain* EVIL. And besides, I have, in every stage of the war, shown a disposition to overlook political weaknesses, conceiving that every man we could retain in the service an acquisition, tending to draw forth the whole strength and abilities of my country against the common enemy.

That the conversation alluded to is a new tale, devised in the malignancy of party, has been asserted by you; and on this assertion is founded many of your strongest conclusions in favour of your own innocence. But what must the world think of your effrontery, when they read the following letter of Col. Alexander Hamilton, who was then Aid-de-Camp to the Commander-in-chief, and now a delegate in Congress; whose conduct and character are well known and approved by the citizens of every State in the Union,--a gentleman, who, being a resident of the State of New York, cannot be supposed in any manner concerned in the politics of Pennsylvania?

PHILADELPHIA, *14th March, 1783*.

DEAR SIR:--Though disagreeable to appear in any manner in a personal dispute; yet I cannot, in justice to you, refuse to comply with the request contained in your note. I have delayed answering it, to endeavour to recollect, with more precision, the time, place and circumstances of the conversation, to which you allude. I cannot, however, remember with certainty more than this: that some time in the campaign of seventy-seven, at head-quarters in this State, you mentioned to me and some other gentlemen of General Washington's family, in a confidential way, that at some period in seventy-six, I think after the American army crossed the Delaware in its retreat, Mr. Reed had spoken to you in terms of great despondency respecting American affairs, and had intimated, that he thought it time for gentlemen to take care of themselves, and that it was unwise any longer to follow the fortunes of a ruined cause, or something of a similar import.

It runs in my mind, that the expressions you declared to have
been made use of by Mr. Reed were, that he thought he ought no
longer to "risk his life and fortunes with the shattered
remains of a broken army:" but it is the part of candour to
observe, that I am not able to distinguish with certainty,
whether the recollection I have of these words arises from the
strong impression made by your declaration at the time, or
from having heard them more than once repeated within a year
past.

I am, dear sir, with great esteem, your obedient servant,
A. HAMILTON.
To General Cadwalader.

At the time I communicated the contents of Colonel Hamilton's certificate
to him, in confidence, it appears by your own acknowledgment, that[G] "no
party or prejudices existed, (at least as to you,")--"the intercourse
arising from these mingled duties and services, which were continued until
the army went into winter quarters, at the VALLEY FORGE, soon did away the
coolness which had for some years subsisted, and in no small degree revived
our former habits of friendship;"--"but it was our lot to meet again, a few
days before the battle of Monmouth; here we were again united in confidence
and danger. After the battle, we left the army together, and that period
closed our friendly intercourse forever." From these, (your expressions,)
you affect to believe, and wish the world to think, that our former
friendship was restored. It was not so; I cannot call it friendship. The
transaction I have mentioned occasioned the dissolution of that intimacy,
contracted in early life, which but little accorded with my notion of
perfect integrity. From that time, and owing solely to that cause, I took
the resolution to avoid your company, as a private gentleman, and which I
constantly adhered to. Meeting in the army, where we served most of the
time in the character of volunteers, I did not think it right to suffer

former dislikes to interrupt the duties and services required of us by the commander-in-chief, so necessary for mutual and general safety. If, then, my dislike to you did not proceed from such motives as sometimes induce men to seek for opportunities of gratifying their resentments, for what purpose could I have invented such a "***tale***?" or if my resentment was such as you represent, why did I not gratify it by making it public immediately? at that time, my mind could not have been "inflamed by party;" because you admit, that no parties then existed, ("at least as to you;") nor could my ambition have been disappointed,--because, being commanding officer of the Pennsylvania Militia, (the council of safety, who then held the powers of government,) could not gratify me further. I could not have "mistaken a conversation with some other person," because there was not that "distance of time," which you suppose, nor can it be conceived by the most credulous to be "some jocular expression;" because the situation of affairs rather suppressed than excited in you the appearance of mirth. Having mentioned this conversation long before parties were formed here, it must appear to every impartial person, that it could not have been the mere invention of my own "brain," suggested in the spirit of party; and it is still more absurd to suppose, that I could have foreseen that you, who then thought as I did concerning the essential objections to the constitution of Pennsylvania, should refuse the appointment of Chief Justice, because you could not, in conscience, take the oath of office; that Mr. Wharton (the first President,) should die; and yet that you should afterwards accept the chair of government. It is, however, incontestibly proved, that the conversation alluded to was spoken of by me at an early period, and long before your appointment to the chair of government; and yet you say, "the prosecution of General Arnold, I have no doubt, gave rise to it." If I was to leave it to your ingenuity to explain to the world my motives for inventing such a "tale," to what purposes could you possibly impute my design? It could not be to gratify my resentment for the injury you attempted upon my property; because I did not then make it public; it could not be occasioned by any personal offence taken in 1777, (when I privately mentioned it to Colonel Hamilton,) because you contend that our "former habits of friendship" were revived, and acknowledge, that I never made it public for several years afterwards. Here, then, the man of humanity may ask me, why did you, at so late a date, publicly mention a circumstance injurious to General Reed's reputation, as adjutant-general of the army and a patriot, which after-services ought to have consigned to oblivion? The question is a natural one, and I will give it an answer. The first occasion of my mentioning this matter publicly was this: soon after our return to the city, in the year 1778, among the victims selected for public examples, there was a young gentleman, with whom I had formed an intimacy in early life. I considered him, as he was by many, (and his acquittal justified the opinion,) as unjustly persecuted; but General Reed, who had resumed his original profession, ***voluntarily*** aided the prosecution, and with all the force of declamation, labored to inflame his judges and jury against him. It was then, recollecting how near he once appeared to the commission of the same offence which he charged upon the other, or at least to a defection from the cause, that my indignation broke out at the trial, saying to those around me, that "***it argued the extremity of effrontery and baseness, in one man to pursue another to death, for taking a step which his own foot had been once raised to take***!"[H] This was anterior to his elevation to the Presidency, and whilst his powers of doing mischief, were he so inclined, were circumscribed by the narrowness of his sphere of action; at such a time, could I think his loss of fame so essential to the public good, or, if he will, to the purposes of party, as to be willing to attempt it, at the expense of my private veracity, my honour and conscience.

The inconsistency of such ostensible conduct, and the baseness of a meditated defection, is not irreconcilable to those who have had opportunities of knowing that he is not incapable of such vast extremes; who have seen him at the bar of the assembly he himself disqualified by the non-compliance with the test of laws, as since fully appears by a publication signed Sidney, unblushingly attempt to set aside the famous Chester election, upon the suggestion of its having been carried by electors disqualified from the like circumstances.

It is thus I would have answered the question, why I have mentioned publicly your meditated defection, and I trust that such provocation merited those reflections which might otherwise have remained in my own breast.

The objection to the force of my single testimony thus obviated, did no other offer to corroborate it, I should not hesitate to submit it, under such circumstances, to the judgment of the public, resting *their* determination upon the credit of *my* veracity against *yours*. Having supported an unblemished character, I dare defy any person to produce an instance where I have even been suspected of an untruth, or of a base or dishonourable action. Conscious of the truth of what I have asserted, I have no fears that my conduct will ever "dishonour me with the wise and virtuous."

The reason I have assigned for the dissolution of our intimacy antecedent to the war, will afford a better proof of your ingenuity than your integrity; and further, (with respect to your veracity,) if any other instance is necessary, let me add one which happened at camp, (at head-quarters,) in the year 1777, soon after the battle of Germantown, when in my hearing, and in the presence of three officers of the first rank in the army, you was charged to your face with a falsehood, and which was fully proved the next day, by the general officer who made the charge.

And now, before I introduce the concurrent testimony in support of my assertion, I shall take but a momentary notice here of those disrespectful expressions with which you have decorated your pamphlet. Weakness of head, is an accusation of a kind which it would equally puzzle the fool and the wise to reply to; but against that of badness of heart, my known tenor of conduct, in private and public life, must be my defence; if that fails, it must be needless in me to set up any other.

But if even prejudiced men should still doubt the truth of my assertion, with respect to the conversation alluded to, in the above representation, every doubt must be removed upon reading the following certificates.

Hermitage, 5th October, 1782.

DEAR GENERAL,--In the winter of 1776, after we had crossed the Delaware, General Reed, in conversation with me, said that he, and several others of my friends, were surprised at seeing me there. I told him, I did not understand such a conversation; that as I had engaged in the cause from principle, I was determined to share the fate of my country; to which he made no reply, and the conversation ended. As I had the honour of commanding the militia of New Jersey, both duty and inclination led me to use every exertion, in support of a cause I had engaged in from the purest motives. I was really much surprised at General Reed's manner, considering the station he then acted in, and his reputation as a patriot; but I considered it as the effect of despondency, from the then gloomy prospect of our affairs.

This I mentioned to several of my friends at the time, who all viewed it in the same point of light.

I am, dear General, yours,

General Cadwalader. P. DICKINSON.

I do hereby certify, that in December, 1776, while the militia lay at Bristol, General Reed, to the best of my recollection and belief, upon my inquiring the news, and what he thought of our affairs in general, said that appearances were very gloomy and unfavourable; that he was fearful or apprehensive the business was nearly settled, or the game almost up, or words to the same effect. That these sentiments appeared to me very extraordinary and dangerous, as I conceived they would, at *that time*, have a very bad tendeney, if publicly known to be the sentiments of General Reed, who then held an appointment in the army of the first consequence.

Philadelphia, March 12, 1783.   JOHN DIXON.

A few days before the battle of Trenton, on the 26th of December, 1776, I rode with Mr. Reed from Bristol to Head Quarters near New Town. In the course of our ride, our conversation turned upon public affairs, when Mr. Reed expressed himself in the manner following.

He spoke with great respect of the bravery of the British troops, and with great contempt of the cowardice of the American, and more especially of the New England troops. So great was the terror inspired by the British soldiers into the minds of our men, that he said, when a British soldier was brought as a prisoner to our camp, our soldiers viewed him at a distance as a superior kind of being.

Upon my lamenting to him the supposed defection of Mr. Dickinson, who it was unjustly said, had deserted his country, he used the following words: "Damn him--I wish the devil had him, when he wrote the Farmer's letters. He has began an opposition to Great Britain which we have not strength to finish."

Upon my lamenting that a gentleman, of his acquaintance, had submitted to the enemy, he said, "that he had acted properly, and that a man who had a family, did right to take that care of them."

The whole of his conversation upon the subject of our affairs, indicated a great despair of the American cause.

Upon my going to Baltimore, to take my seat in Congress, the latter end of January, I mentioned the above conversation to my brother. I likewise mentioned it to the Hon. John Adams, Esq., with whom I then lived in intimacy, a day or two after his return from Boston to Congress. I did not mention it with a view of injuring Mr. Reed, for I still respected him, especially as I then believed that the victory at Trenton had restored the tone of his mind, and dissipated his fears, but to show Mr. Adams an instance of a man possessing and exercising military spirit and activity, and yet deficient in political fortitude. To which I well remember Mr. Adams replied in the following words: "The powers of the human mind are combined together in an infinite variety of ways."

BENJAMIN RUSH.

Philadelphia, March 3, 1783.

I went with Congress to Baltimore, in 1776. On the arrival of my brother there, a few weeks afterwards, I called to see him. To the best of my recollection, Mr. Clerk and Dr. Witherspoon, delegates from New Jersey, were in the room with him. The two former, after some time withdrew, and my brother then mentioned the conversation as related by him above. He informed me, also, of some *other* conversation that passed between Mr. Reed and him, which is not necessary at present to repeat.

JACOB RUSH.

Philadelphia, March 3, 1783.

Joseph Ellis, a Colonel of Militia, in the county of Gloucester, and State of New Jersey, doth hereby certify, that upon the retreat of a body of militia from before Count Donop, in the neighborhood of Mount Holly, in Burlington county, in the month of December, 1776, he met with Charles Pettit, Esq., *then Secretary of the said State*, that a conversation ensued between them respecting the situation of the public dispute at that period; that Mr. Pettit, in said conversation, representing that our affairs were desperate, Col. Ellis endeavoured to dissuade him from such an opinion, when Mr. Pettit replied, "What hurts me more than all is, my brother-in-law, General Reed, has, (or I believe he has,) given up the contest." That a good deal more passed between Mr. Pettit and Col. Ellis, during the said cnnversation, but omitted here, as being thought unnecessary.

JOSEPH ELLIS.

Woodbury, March 9, 1783.

I do certify that I was present at the conversation alluded to above; that although I cannot recollect the express words made use of in the said conversation, yet such conversation did take place, and that the substance of it answers to the certificate of Col. Ellis.

FRANKLIN DAVENPORT.

Woodbury, March 9, 1783.

These are to certify, that in December, 1776, and January, 1777, I, the subscriber, was Major of the second battalion of Philadelphia Militia, whereof John Bayard was Colonel, and then lay at Bristol, and part of the time opposite Trenton, on the Pennsylvania side. That while we lay at Bristol, Joseph Reed, Esq., joined us; that during his being there and near Trenton, he often went out for intelligence, as Col. Bayard told me, over to Burlington, in which place the enemy frequently were; that being absent frequently all day and all night, I as frequently inquired what could become of Gen. Reed. Col. Bayard often answered me, he feared he had left us and gone over to the enemy. One time in particular, being absent two days and two nights, if not three nights, Col. Bayard came to me with great concern, and said he was fully persuaded Gen. Reed was gone to join the enemy and make his peace. I asked him, how he could possibly think so of a man, who had taken so early a part, and had acted steadily. He replied, he was persuaded it was so; for he knew the General thought it was all over, and that we would not stand against the enemy; and at the same time wept much. I endeavoured all I could to drive such notions from him, but he was so fully persuaded that he had left us and gone over to the enemy, that arguing about the matter was only loss of time; Col. Bayard often making mention, that he knew his sentiments much better than I did. After being absent two or three nights, Gen. Reed returned, and I never saw more joy expressed than was by Col. Bayard; he declared to me, that he was glad Gen. Reed was returned, for he was fully convinced in his own mind that he was gone over to the enemy.

WILLIAM BRADFORD.

Manor of Moreland, Philadelphia County, March 15, 1783.

Having been called upon by General Cadwalader respecting a report which has been propagated concerning Mr. Joseph Reed--I declare on my honour, the circumstances are as follows. In the spring of 1780, I obtained permission for an interview with my brother at Elizabethtown. In the course of conversation, one day, he happened to mention that there were men among us, who held the first offices, who applied for protection from the British while they lay in New Jersey. I was alarmed at this assertion, and insisted on knowing who they were;--he said, that when the British army lay in Jersey, in 1776, Count Donop commanded at Bordentown; that he was often at that officer's quarters, and possessed some degree of his confidence; that one day, an inhabitant came into their lines, with an application from Mr. Joseph Reed, the purport of which was, to know whether he could have protection for himself and his property, (there was another person included in the *application*, whose *name* it is not necessary here to mention.) The man was immediately ordered for execution, but it was prevented by the interposition of my brother and some other persons, who had formerly known him. Perhaps Mr. Reed and his friends may say, that Count Donop would not have ordered the man executed, had he not thought he came for intelligence. No doubt that officer would have justified his conduct by putting upon the footing of a spy, but why was another person included in the application, and one who was not looked on as a trifling character? his name I will mention to any one who will apply to me; however, my brother said, the man who was sent with the application was a poor peasant, and the most unfit person in the world to send for intelligence; this argument was what had weight with Count Donop, and which saved his life.[I] These circumstances being mentioned by a brother, and which he declared to be true, naturally produced an alteration in my sentiments of Mr. Reed; for previous to this, there were few men of whom I entertained so high an opinion. On my return to Philadelphia, I made no secret of what I heard; indeed, I thought it my duty to mention it publicly, that it might prevent further power being put into the hands of a man who might make a bad use of it. The report circulated daily, and I was often called on to mention the circumstances, which I always did, and which I should have done to Mr. Reed, had he applied to me. I remember, among the number who came to me, was Major Thomas Moore, who said he intended to inform Mr. Reed; but whether he did or not, I cannot pretend to say.

There is another thing I wish to mention. My brother came into the river in a flag of truce, on special application of our commissary of prisoners, to take a number of prisoners who were exchanged, to save us the expense and trouble of sending them by land; this was in the month of May, 1781. He was detained, about nine miles below the city, upwards of four weeks, and never permitted to visit it, although application was made for that purpose, by several captains of vessels, who had been prisoners, and to whom he had rendered civilities. I declined making application myself, as I supposed my being in the service from the commencement of the war, and having endured a rigorous confinement for eighteen months, in the worst of times, to have been sufficient to have obtained permission for a brother to have been in my house, in preference to a cabin in a small vessel in a river;--however,

I endeavoured to make his situation as agreeable as possible, by visiting him often, and by taking my friends with me. I REMEMBER Col. Francis Nichols went with me one day, to whom my brother mentioned Mr. Reed's intended desertion, and who, I doubt not, will acknowledge it, on any person's applying to him; he is at present in Virginia, but is expected in town in a few days.

DAVID LENNOX.

Having been called upon by General Cadwalader, to certify, so far as my knowledge extends, as to the matter hereinafter mentioned, I do declare, that in the spring of the year 1781, I went with Major Lennox, of this city, on board of a flag of truce vessel, then lying in the river Delaware, where she had arrived from New York, and heard Mr. Robert Lennox, deputy commissary of prisoners under the British king, say, that in the year of 1776, a person had arrived at Count Donop's quarters, near Bordentown, in New Jersey, who told the Count, that he had been sent to him by Gen. Reed and another person, whose name I do not think necessary to mention, to procure a protection for them; that the Count refused to grant them a protection in that manner, and was about to treat the person who had applied to him as a spy, but was prevented by the entreaties of the said Robert Lennox, and some other gentlemen.

Philadelphia, 17th March, 1783. FRANCIS NICHOLS.

Here, then, it fully appears, that the testimony contained in the above certificates, all point to the same object, and to the same period mentioned by me, supporting and confirming each other. They likewise clearly prove the whole progress of your meditated defection; they prove that you deceived me by those professions, by which I had been induced to trust to your appearances of fidelity, as you absolutely made an application for a protection to Count Donop, in which an intimate friend of yours was included.

But what opinion must the world form of your veracity, when you are detected in falsely asserting, that you had not mentioned such sentiments to your most intimate friends and relations. "Is it not utterly incredible," you say, "that I should hold such communication or sentiments from my most intimate friends and relations, and make it to a person with whom I had held no friendship for many years; who had received me with coldness." Mr. Pettit is your relation, and Col. Bayard your most intimate friend, with whom, at that time, you had the freest intercourse. To these you communicated your sentiments, as appears by the certificates of Col. Bradford, Col. Ellis, and Mr. Davenport; but your friend, hinted at in Major Lennox's certificate, had consented to accompany you in your intended desertion. The height of your iniquity does not end here; you endeavoured, by your influence, to spread general disaffection, in order to lessen your share of the infamy, by dividing it among many. Had you conferred with men whose principles were in every instance like your own, you might have succeeded, as every person concerned might have carried off his particular friend with him.

If all the evidence which now appears against you, had been produced at that time, what would have been your fate, as you then, (being ***Adjutant-General*** of the army,) was subject to the Continental articles of war?

In the 10th page you say, you can "truly declare, that the subject of the present slander was not known to you, till its appearance in the newspaper." Having mentioned it at the Coffee House, (as appears by Mr. Pryor's certifiate,) in the presence of some of your friends, it was reasonable to expect they would have informed you of it; but it seems there is some difference between private information and a public charge made in the papers. As a gentleman, there can, in my opinion, be no difference; as you say, in your letter of the 9th Sept. last, that this insinuation seems to deserve some credit from a *reference* to *me*. You insinuate, that if you had heard it, you should have noticed it. To this, however, the world will give little credit, as you made no public or private inquiry respecting the charge made in Major Lennox's certificate, though he communicated it to Major Thomas Moore, son of the late President, whose permission I have for asserting publicly, that he informed you of what Major Lennox had related, the very day he heard it.

The matters mentioned in Major Lennox's certificate, and in that of Col. Nichols reach vastly beyond me; here you absolutely apply for protection; and if one report demanded your notice, in reference to my authorities, why not another, more alarming to you, your notice in reference to Major Lennox?

But the consciousness of the communications made to confidential friends, and others, suggested the fear of other proofs. As long as it was only communicated by private information, you were willing to submit to private censure. But when a charge, which originated from me, was made in the papers, it reduced you to the disagreeable alternative of a tacit confession, or the hazard of public proof. And in the present instance, if I am rightly informed, you was perfectly disposed to treat the publication signed Brutus, with that "silent contempt," which, you say, you have for a "long time observed, with respect to the anonymous abuse which disgraces our public papers;" but your friends, feeling the weight of the charge, goaded you into so unfortunate a measure. *"Unhappy man! against whose peace and happiness all are combined."*

What answer can you make to the weight of testimony here produced against you? I see nothing left, but to declare to the world, that the whole is a wicked combination to destroy you; you may say, "you thought *me* entitled to the whole infamy of the insinuation," till the above mentioned witnesses "consented to divide it with me;" and that, "if you did not sufficiently measure the malignancy of their dispositions, or thought more favourably of them than you ought to have done, you are content to acknowledge your error, and do full justice in this respect hereafter;" and if any person should ask you, would all these gentlemen hazard such assertions without foundation? you may answer, "it is difficult to resolve what men of ungovernable passions will or will not say, when their minds are inflamed by party, and their breasts burning with disappointed ambition;" may they not have "mistaken a conversation with some other person, or at this distance of time, converted some JOCULAR EXPRESSION into such suspicions as they have mentioned;" and you may add, "the MEMORIES of MEN may fail; their minds are subject to the warp of prejudice and passion; they may convert into serious import what was dropped in JEST; and, from false pride, persist in what they have said, because they have said it, even against the conviction of their own consciences."

In your letter of the 23d of September last, you say, "you have declared the insinuations in Oswald's paper of the 7th inst. false; and you apply the same epithet to my avowal of them." This assertion has been fully refuted by the concurrent testimony of your *intimate friends* and others. In your friends, you thought yourself perfectly secure; but the weakness of two of them has betrayed you, and the third is proved your accomplice.

It would, indeed, have appeared somewhat extraordinary, if you had not discovered your intentions to some of your intimate friends and relations; and that "no circumstance should occur to correspond with this imputation," after having communicated the same to me. Nor are proofs wanting, if they were here necessary, independently of those I have already adduced, with respect to some of your friends, who at the time held considerable commands in the militia.

And "though specially sent by General Washington," as you say, "for the express purpose of assisting me," it may not be here improper to make a short observation, in which I conceive I shall be perfectly justifiable. Though the duties of an Adjutant General would naturally confine you to the Continental army, yet I can easily conceive that there was no difficulty, by hints thrown out, or by the interposition of a friend, to induce the commander-in-chief to permit you to come to Bristol, under the *pretence* of assisting me; being, as *you represent*, well acquainted with the inhabitants of Burlington, through whom you might obtain information. But from the evidence which appears against you, it will not be thought uncharitable to conclude, that you conceived your plan could be better executed at Bristol, than under the eye of General Washington. Besides, you might reasonably hope to shake more easily the constancy of untried officers of militia, than those in the army, whose minds might be supposed better fortified against such attacks.

I am at a loss for words to express my indignation for the attempt you made on my integrity; for though I did not see it in that point of view at the time, yet the whole testimony, as now collected, fully proves such to have been your intention; and happy I conceive it to be for my own honour and the safety of my country, that you found in me that strength of mind, which you might not have experienced in some of your particular friends, had they been in my situation.

The circumstances relating to the letter you wrote Count Donop, created at the time no suspicions; nor do I recollect any publication which alludes to it. This affair, and that mentioned by Major Lenox, are distinct transactions; but it is not more than probable, that at the interview you proposed under cover of serving the inhabitants of Burlington, you intended to confer with Count Donop upon the subject of your own interest and personal safety? This suspicion, in my opinion, is perfectly warranted by the indubitable proofs of your intended desertion. Another circumstance relating to this affair was equally unusual and improper. Mr. Daniel

Ellis,[J] by whom you sent the letter with a flag, was universally known to be disaffected; having been so long in the service you could not be ignorant of those obvious reasons, which prove the propriety of sending men with flags, whose attachment to the cause is well known, and men of observation.

Every page, almost, of your publication is full of reflections against me, and almost upon every subject; so intent have you been to injure my reputation. The errors I committed during my command may serve a double purpose; because he who committed them is subject to censure, and he who points them out claims the merit of the discovery. That I committed errors, I readily admit; my friends have marked some, and subsequent experience discovered others; but I am conscious they proceed from want of experience, not a want of integrity. Why, then, need I seek to justify myself, when, from the nature of the war, considerable commands were, from necessity, entrusted to young officers, there being few amongst us to whom the profession was not entirely new. But, I confess, it would give me infinite pain, if, by "a strange inattention of mine to the tide and state of the river," and the not arriving "one hour" sooner at Dunk's Ferry, we had lost the opportunity of striking a blow at Mount Holly, of equal glory with that at Trenton. When you insinuated, in the former part of your address, a superior knowledge in military matters, by saying you had more "experience," I gave up the point, and left you the happiness of thinking so; for why should I have contended a point with a man who, throughout his pamphlet, assumes to himself the merit of all those brilliant successes, so highly commended even by our enemies, and which determined the fate of American independence. And if I was sensible that the charge you now make was true, or could be thought so, by competent judges, I would scorn to defend my error.

My orders were, to make the attack one hour before day, and to effect a surprise, if possible. The impropriety, therefore, of sending the boats from Bristol to Dunk's Ferry, and marching the troops from the same place in open day, is evident, as such a movement must have been observed, and communicated to the enemy. And now, tell me the instance, where even continental troops have arrived at the point of attack at the given time? It was General Washington's intention to have made his attack on Trenton before day; yet, from unavoidable delays, he did not arrive there till after eight o'clock in the morning. We reached Dunk's Ferry a little before low water, and can any person believe, that if we had arrived "one hour sooner," we could have passed over near twenty-five hundred men, four pieces of cannon, ammunition wagons and horses, and all the horses belonging to officers, in that time, in the night too, and the river full of ice, with only five large batteauxs and two or three scows; when it took us at least six hours, (a day or two afterwards,) to cross above Bristol, in open day and the river almost clear of ice. Strange "inattention," unhappy commander! That "*a single hour*, which we might have enjoyed with equal convenience and equal risk," should be the only obstacle to a scene of equal glory with that of Trenton, and yet you have represented to General Washington, as appears by his letter,[K] dated six o'clock, P. M., 25th December, 1776, to me, ***being the very same night***, and before we marched to Dunk's Ferry, that you gave him the most discouraging accounts of what might be expected from our operations below. What, then, were those discouraging accounts? Why was I not acquainted with them? or were they thrown out to influence him from making his attempt on Trenton, by representing that no co-operation from our quarter could favour his enterprise? In the general's opinion, it is plain, it had that tendency. But in the heedless fury of this stroke at me, you have incautiously unguarded your most tender part.

"Anxious to fill up the part of this glorious plan assigned to us," you "passed over, you say, with your horse, to see and judge for yourself." You did so. "Having seen the last man re-embarked, you proceeded before day to Burlington." Here permit me to correct you, because there is no circumstance better ascertained, than that many of the men were not brought back till eight o'clock the next morning.

Your motives for going to Burlington that night, were then thought a mystery; 'tis now no longer so; and the "*other circumstances*," that permitted you to join us again at Bristol, are now clearly accounted for. General Washington's success or defeat was, no doubt, to determine whether you were to remain a citizen of the United States of America, or to be a shameful deserter of your country.

You say, you went to Philadelphia, at my request, to confer with Gen. Putnam; that you set out in the evening, (the 24th December,) and reached Philadelphia about midnight; but what credit, can you reasonably expect, will be given to your "detail of proceedings," in other particulars, when you find yourself detected in such gross contradictions in the following instance?

In the 17th page you say, "Upon conference with General Putnam, (at Philadelphia,) he represented the state of the militia, the general confusion which prevailed, his apprehensions of an insurrection in the city in his absence, and many other circumstances, in such strong terms, as convinced me, no assistance could be derived from him;" and yet, in your letter to me, dated Philadelphia, 25th December, 1776, 11 o'clock, you say; "General Putnam has determined to cross the river, with as many men as he can collect, which, he says, will be about five hundred; he is now mustering them, and endeavouring to get Proctor's company of artillery to go with them. I wait to know what success he meets with, and the progress he makes; but, at all events, I shall be with you this afternoon."

Here the representation stated in your pamphlet is contradicted by a letter in your own handwriting. Having forgot, perhaps, that you had written such a letter, your ingenuity furnished materials for a plausible narrative, suitable to your purposes; not suspecting that such proof could be adduced in opposition to it.

Having returned to Bristol about daylight on the 26th December, with the greater part of the troops, I received an account, about 11 o'clock, A. M., from a person just arrived from Trenton Ferry, that General Washington had succeeded in his attack. I immediately despatched a messenger with a line to General Ewing, for information, but all I could learn was, that the victory was ours.

From the continuance of the rain and wind, I concluded the ice must be destroyed in the course of the day, and instantly sent down to Dunk's Ferry for the boats. This being an extraordinary service, required of men who had been exposed to the storm the whole night, was, however, cheerfully undertaken and executed. I then consulted Col. Hitchcock, who commanded the
New England brigade, to know whether his troops would willingly accompany us to New Jersey, as I had determined to cross the river in the morning, if practicable, to co-operate with General Washington. He informed me, that his troops could not march, unless they could be supplied with shoes, stockings and breeches; upon which I instantly wrote to the Council of Safety, and obtained seven hundred pairs of each of the above articles, which arrived about sunrise on the morning of the 27th December. This second attempt being determined on, I went with several officers, in the afternoon of the 26th, to fix upon a proper place for crossing the river above Bristol, and the next morning before day viewed the Jersey Shore in a barge, for the same purpose. By your relation, one would imagine you had been the *life and soul* of this second movement across the Delaware,--as little privy to it as the emperor of Morocco,--but it is no unusual thing for you to intercept the praise due to others of creditable actions.
Instead of being present to confirm my proposed movements, by your advice, you remained at Burlington, "in a kind of concealment, till the weather and OTHER CIRCUMSTANCES permitted you to join us at Bristol," after all our resolutions were taken, and the most of our arrangements made. In the tissue of your representations, it is your purpose to insinuate my deficiency in military conduct in the subsequent transactions. Let my

relation of it be heard!

We marched on the 27th, in the morning, and the ice being by this time chiefly destroyed, we met with little obstruction in passing. The last division of the troops being embarked, and then crossing, we received private information, that General Washington had re-crossed the river, and returned to Newtown, in Pennsylvania, from whence he dates his letter, 27th December, 1776, informing me of the particulars of the action at Trenton, and which was not received, contrary to your assertion, till we had marched above a mile on our way to Burlington; it was then read to the troops, who were halted for this purpose. We had, however, before given full credit to the first information of his having re-crossed; on which previous information I called together the field officers, to consult what was then best to be done. From this circumstance, Col. Hitchcock, and some others, proposed returning to Bristol. I instantly declared my determination against it, and recommended an attack upon Mount Holly, as from the information we had of the force at that post, we might easily carry it, and should then have a retreat open towards Philadelphia, if necessary. You then, "*as a middle course*," advised our going to Burlington; in which those who had at first proposed our return, joined in opinion. This was the true cause of that hesitation you remarked with respect to me. Burlington was in a position, in my judgment, very dangerous; as in case we should be invested there, and the river impassable, we should be forced to submit at discretion, for want of provisions, or hazard an action against troops superior in discipline, and perhaps in number, if their whole force was collected to that point. Having no other retreat open to us, but that over the river, it was evident this could not be effected without the loss, at least, of those who might be ordered to cover the retreat. Having passed the river in open day, it was probable the enemy might be informed of it; and, in that case, the post at Mount Holly reinforced. To determine whether we should take a position, unanimously approved by the council, but which I thought extremely dangerous; or adhere to my own plan, unsupported by a single voice, was certainly a question that required more than a momentary

consideration, even for an officer, at this stage of the war. Being pressed
for some resolution, as the day was far spent, I waived my own opinion, and
acquiesced in the desire of marching to Burlington; but it is ridiculous to
suppose, as you say, that your brother's intelligence of Count Donop's
retreat, could have influenced my acquiescence, for it did not arrive till
after our resolutions were taken,--and besides, was not credited; because
if it had reached us before, and been credited, I should not have
acquiesced in such desire; if even after, I should naturally have taken
another course, and pursued the flying enemy, instead of going to
Burlington, which was five miles in the rear.

Late that night, I received certain information, that the enemy had
evacuated all their posts in the neighborhood, and immediately despatched a
messenger to General Washington with the intelligence; in answer to which,
I received his orders, very early next morning, to pursue and keep up the
panic, and that he would cross at Trenton that day. From this circumstance,
it appears that the General had taken his determination before your
pretended information or advice from Trenton could have reached him.

In justification to myself, I have thought it necessary to point out your
false state of facts, in these particulars; the multitude of lesser ones,
relating to military matters, I shall pass over, as this publication is
already necessarily lengthened beyond my first intention.

As I hinted, in my letter of 10th September last, that "charges of the same
nature had been, some time since, made against you," by Arnold; you say,
you "allow full weight to so respectable a connexion and testimony;" to
which you made no reply, though from the rank and character of Arnold at
that time, they merited your notice. Arnold having received his information
from me, it cannot be concluded, that I meant by his testimony to
strengthen my own assertion; but merely to show, that having before been
charged, you did not reply; from which many believed it true. And when he
apologized to me for inserting it in his defence without my permission, I

remarked, that an apology was unnecessary, from the public manner in which I had mentioned it.

Arnold was commanding officer in this city, very generally visited by officers of the army, citizens and strangers. I received the usual civilities from him, and returned them; and often met him at the tables of gentlemen in the city. To my civilities, at that time, I thought him entitled from the signal services he had rendered his country; services infinitely superior to those you so much boast of; he stood high, as a military character, even in France, and after your prosecution, he was continued in command by Congress; appointed first, by the commander-in-chief, to the command of the left wing of the army, and afterwards to that important post of West Point, where his treacherous conduct exceeded, I fancy, even your own idea of his baseness. To what, then, do your insinuations amount? They cannot criminate me, without an implied censure on Congress and the commander-in-chief. But why contaminate
my name, by connecting it, in this instance, with such a wretch? when you, yourself, at his trial, with a half-shamed face, seemed to apologize for being his prosecutor, and became his fulsome panegyrist. It consisted, however, with that artifice and cunning which has ever been the sum of your *abilities*, and the whole amount of your *wisdom*.

Your remarks on my letter of the 10th December, 1777, are so inconsistent, that I shall bestow a few observations on them. "So strong and virulent," you say, "was my antipathy to the constitution, and such my enmity to those who administered it, that you believe I would have preferred *any* government to that of Pennsylvania, if my *person* and *property* would have been equally secure;" and yet it seems, in the next sentence you say, "but it was our lot to meet again, a few days before the battle of Monmouth; here we were again united in *confidence* and *danger*." If you really thought I would prefer *any government* to that of Pennsylvania, why did you then take so much pains to show, that we again united in "*confidence* and *danger*," at the battle of Monmouth, so many months after I had discovered that virulent antipathy, and which now hath extorted such gross reflections?

You say, my breast was burning with disappointed ambition; but how does this appear, when, immediately upon the formation of the new government, I was appointed the first of three brigadiers, which created me commanding officer of the militia. Could my ambition be gratified further? But to obviate every objection, let me suppose you meant, that I wished to rise to power in the civil line,--which, however, has never been insinuated before,--let me here call to your memory, how easy the task was for *any character* to rise to the first offices of government. I confess, I do not think so meanly of myself, as to have dreaded any rivalship from some of the candidates of those days; nor do I mean, by this declaration, to insinuate any extraordinary merit, when I estimate mine by that of those I have alluded to. I could not have consented to make the sacrifices required; but you, however, and some others, as much opposed to the essential parts of the constitution as I was, freely made them, and broke through every obligation of faith and honour.

The charge you have brought against a party in the state, of an opposition to its constitution, deserves some attention. I will digress a little from my main subject to examine how far this charge is true, and how far the thing is in itself criminal.

Government is generally so reverenced among men, that those who attempt to subvert any system of it whatever, have to contend against a very natural prejudice. But this prejudice can only be in degree with the antiquity of its establishment; for modern error, how high soever its authority, has but little claim to our veneration. This concession made, could it be expected that our novel constitution, liable at first blush to so many important objections, should not have its opponents; but that in a moment it should be submitted to, as implicitly as if it had had the sanction of ages? What circumstance was there, in the production of this whimsical machine, that should silence, at once, all the remonstrances of reason and sense against it? Was it not worth a pause to examine, whether this coat, wove for ages, would fit us or our posterity before we put on; or whether this gift of our convention would not prove our destruction? From an apprehension that it would, an opposition was formed, that included a majority of the state. Did those who composed it, think it criminal to prevent the singular ideas of a convention, from being carried into execution, against an almost general sentiment; or did they not rather conceive it safe and better for the community still to go on in the administration of governmental affairs by those temporary expedients we had been in the habits of, until their constitution could be revised?

This idea, patriotic as it was, was defeated by the obstinate enthusiasm of some, who trembled for this New Jerusalem of their hopes, and by the scandalous desertion of others, and especially yourself. The ends of opposition being thus rendered unattainable, but at the hazard of convulsions, that might endanger the great American cause, the same virtue that began it, ended it, and it has long since ceased to act.

This is a well-known state of facts; but what it did not suit with your own by-purposes to admit, could not be expected from your integrity; you have, therefore, constantly kept up the alarm of a constitutional opposition, and, on every occasion, referred to this false cause, that honest and useful opposition which was created by your weak, though violent and tyrannical administration.

That you was called to the chair of government, by the unanimous vote of council and assembly, you have often boasted, with a view of conveying to the world an idea, that even the gentlemen opposed to the constitution approved the choice. But they neither esteemed you as a gentleman, nor approved your public conduct. They knew there was a majority in assembly in favour of your election, and as their grand object was the obtaining a resolution of that body, recommending the calling a convention for revising the constitution, some of the party entered into an engagement for this purpose, and your election was negotiated. ***You*** were to use your endeavours to prevail on the Council to enforce the recommendation of the assembly by a similar resolution. From your own acknowledgment at the City Tavern, the resolution of the Council was never obtained, or even moved for, by you, and for this flimsy reason, that no formal information, of such resolution having passed, had been communicated to you; though known to all the world; and that it could not be expected that Council would "tag" after the assembly, in a measure relating to the public. Yet you had the effrontery to assert, that "***every engagement on your part***," was strictly performed.

At this meeting, you say, you "in the most open manner called upon us, to support our imputations, and that you so effectually vindicated every part of your conduct, that every gentleman, (myself excepted,) acknowledged his mistake." I own I made no concessions, and if the reasons I then gave are not thought a sufficient justification to the world, of the opinion I had formed, I am content to admit that it was not only "singular," but "absurd."

After a reasonable pause, I remarked, that from the repeated conversations I had had with you, on this subject, you appeared to me as much opposed as I was, to the constitution, before the evacuation of the city; that you had refused to accept the appointment of Chief Justice, (because you could not in conscience take the oath;[L]) that a short time before the election, in 1778, you engaged yourself to the constitutional party, to serve in Council for the County, and to the party in the opposition, to serve in Assembly for the City; and being chosen in both instances, you hesitated above six weeks, (though often pressed to a resolution,) before you determined to accept your seat in Council;--depriving, during this time, the City of a vote in Assembly, while an important point was debated concerning the contested Chester election; and voluntarily advocating the question in favor of the constitutional party; that on the fate of this trial depended your hopes of succeeding to the President's chair; that a determination in favour of that party gave them a decided majority, and that you instantly accepted your seat in Council.--To which you replied, and in recapitulating my arguments, endeavoured to justify your conduct; but conscious of having failed in the capital points, you closed your remarks with some warm expressions, which conveyed the idea of a threat; of which I desired an explanation. After working up your passions to a degree little short of frenzy, you expressed yourself in the following terms: I mean this,--"If the publications traducing my public and private character are continued, I mean to apply to the law; but if this will not do me that justice, which in some instances it cannot do,--I know I have the affections and command of the fighting men of this state; and if necessary, I will make use of that influence, and call forth that force,--and if bloodshed should be the consequence be it on your own heads."

Such violent and unwarrantable expressions from the first magistrate of the state, and in the presence of the whole bench of justices, created the highest indignation, and were severely reprobated by several gentlemen present; which induced you afterwards to endeavour to soften your expressions and meaning.

But if it was singular or absurd, "to expect a President of the State to enter into the violence of party on ***my*** side of the question," let me oppose to this, the ***treachery*** of your conduct in deserting the party to which you was at first from ("***conscientious***" principles) attached, and yet, as President, enter into all the violence of party on the other side of the question.

Again, "upon our return to Philadelphia," you say, "I became the open and avowed patron of those who are distinguished by the appellation of tories; and my decisive attachment to the British Army,[N] and their adherents, "has marked every subsequent period of my life, too plainly to admit of doubt or denial." If you really entertained such sentiments, why did you, in the month of February, (after my marriage,) waiving the indignity offered to you in not paying the usual compliments of congratulation, upon your appointment, pay me the first visit, and thereby make advances towards a reconciliation? Such a condescension, so contrary to the *usual forms*, can scarcely be reconciled even to a character like yours.

Men who acquire popularity by means disgraceful to a gentleman, dare not hazard a sentiment that is not approved by the party with which he is connected. I have, on all occasions, and in all companies, private and public, delivered freely my political opinions; nor has the dread of losing the little popularity I possessed in Pennsylvania, ever induced me to make a sacrifice of my honour, by adopting opinions or measures which I disapproved, or thought injurious to my country. Esteeming it the highest honour to deserve the approbation of my fellow-citizens, I have ever been solicitous to obtain it. You and some others have industriously propagated reports for the purpose of injuring my reputation; but conscious that my political opinions and conduct will stand the test, upon the nicest scrutiny, and having never experienced any diminution of that esteem, respect and warmth of friendship, which my fellow-citizens have ever shown towards me, a refutation of such calumny is utterly needless.

From the whole of what I have here laid before the public, supported by the testimony of the most respectable witnesses, the following conclusions may fairly be deduced:

1. That the conversation alluded to, which I have asserted to have passed between us at Bristol, was mentioned by me in confidence to Col. Hamilton and some others of General Washington's family, in the year 1777; and therefore could not have originated at the time, you mention, or to gratify my resentment against you, as at that time, you acknowledge, no parties subsisted.

2. It could not have been invented to gratify my resentment for the attempt you made to evade the payment of Mr. Porter's order; because I did not make it public at the time, nor till several years afterwards, and you acknowledge, all that coolness was done away, and our former habits of friendship restored.

As is appears, by Mr. Clymer's testimony, that I mentioned it publicly at Mr. Hamilton's trial, which was before you were elected President of the state, it ought to be imputed to another cause than that which you have assigned.

4. As it appears, from Mr. Pryor's testimony, that I mentioned it at the Coffee House, in the hearing of some of your friends, we may reasonably conclude you were informed of it; and this conclusion is strengthened by your passing over unnoticed, the information contained in Major Lennox's testimony, which was related to you by Major Thomas Moore.

5. It cannot appear improbable that you should have held this conversation with me, as your expressions to Gen. Dickinson, Col. Nixon, and Doctor Rush, convey sentiments equally injurious to your reputation as a patriot and Adjutant General of the army.

6. As it fully appears, by the testimony of Col. Ellis and Mr. Davenport, and that of Col. Bradford, that you had communicated such sentiments to your brother-in-law, Mr. Pettit, and to Col. Bayard, contrary to your declaration, we may with propriety assert that you have forfeited that veracity, which is essential to the character of a gentleman.

Lastly, from the testimony of Major Lennox and Col. Nichols, it appears that you absolutely applied to Count Donop for protection, and that a particular and intimate friend of yours was included in it; and therefore, from this and the foregoing testimony, all pointing to the same object and to the same period, supporting and confirming each other, it cannot leave the least room to doubt the truth of my assertion.

In some instances, a man's general good conduct has had great weight to invalidate or weaken charges highly criminal; but unfortunately, **yours** can receive no aid from such circumstances. Dissimulation and cunning have for a time deceived the most discerning, but the snares you have laid for others will most probably accomplish your own destruction.

Having long since known how to estimate your character, I have not any where pretended, in this performance, to fix it at a higher value than what it generally passes current for; you have, since the term of your administration, repeatedly put yourself upon your country. Your name has been offered to the people for a seat in the legislature; to the legislature, for a seat in Congress; to Congress, for posts of Continental trust; but that **name**, its counterfeit gilding at length rubbed off, and the native colour of the contexture exposed, has depreciated, like the Continental money, with such velocity, that though a few years ago worth a President's chair, it would not, **now** purchase a constable's staff; nor is it more highly rated in the sphere of polite life, than in the great theatre of the world; for its unfortunate owner stands alone, unnoticed in the midst of company, with full leisure to reflect on the sensible effects of the loss of reputation.

My immediate purpose requires nothing further from me; but your administration, the theme of your own solitary praise, might not improperly have been touched upon, but that it is a field too extensive for me, and that I have not asperity enough in my nature to do justice to the subject. I will yet observe upon some matters in your pamphlet, not in direct connexion with one or the other subject; but which are extremly demonstrative of a temper in the writer to wish evil to the community, after the power of doing it has ceased.

You, who have ever been a rapacious lawyer, and have never omitted any means of amassing a fortune, have, with a truly consistent spirit, shown an implacable enmity to all those who are raised to a condition above want and dependence. And though you kick against the parallel drawn between you and the Cataline of antiquity, you have in this point proved its exactness; he haranguing in the circle of his conspirators, exasperates them against the opulent citizens of Rome; you, in your pamphlet, labor to create invidious distinctions, would pervert the order of well regulated society, and make fortune's larger gifts, or even its moderate blessings, criterions of disqualification for public trust and honours in Pennsylvania; and under a spacious description of men, offer with your ***sword*** to lead the indigent, the bankrupt, and the desperate, into all the authority of government. But in the shallowness of your understanding, you have mistaken the spirit of the times; it will not countenance or support a Cataline.

You would also, no doubt, as may be inferred from your pamphlet, ***you***, who are so deficient in morality, draw your sword in religious quarrels, to bring you once more into play; but 'tis to no purpose you would raise an alarm, as a very great and respectable part of your opponents consist of persons belonging to that society, of which you profess yourself to be a member; and there is a general and commendable coolness and indifference for such quarrels, that will not easily take fire on your false and inflammatory suggestions; so that whatever you have catched at to raise you from the earth, has broke in your hands and brought you again to the ground.

JOHN CADWALADER.

VALLEY FORGE LETTERS,

AS

PUBLISHED IN THE EVENING JOURNAL.

1842.

From the Evening Journal.

MR. WHITNEY--At this distant day from the American Revolution, a new dawn
seems to be breaking upon the darkness of that period, and much that has
heretofore been shrouded in seemingly inscrutable mystery, is beginning to
be made plain even to the naked vision. The "seventeen trunks" of
revolutionary papers, a selection from which Colonel Beekman, the grandson
and heir of Gen. George Clinton, has just published, in one of the New York
papers, must necessarily contain much of exceeding value: and I should not
be surprised if the Colonel were to receive a visit, at his place on Long
Island, from Mr. William Bradford Reed, to request to be permitted to
rummage their contents, and abstract or destroy any "document" that might
likely prove prejudicial to the fame of his grandfather, the late General
Joseph Reed. The Colonel must keep a sharp look out for Mr. Reed, and turn
a deaf ear to his blandishments, when he arrives.

Doctor Johnson, in one of his Lives of the Poets, makes an observation
strictly applicable to the claim of patriotism, which, originally set up
for himself by General Reed, has been perpetuated for him by his
descendants. Speaking of the boast a certain poet was accustomed to make,

of the sternness with which he had driven back an ass laden with gold, that had sought to invade the citadel of his integrity, the Doctor remarked, "but the tale has too little evidence to deserve a disquisition; ***large offers and sturdy rejections are among the most common topics of falsehood***." That portion of the quotation which I have italicised, fits the case of General Reed to a hair; but "the tale" of his patriotism, however "little evidence" there may to support it, ***does*** "deserve a disquisition," if only on account of the pertinacity with which it is endeavoured to engraft it upon the public mind.

I have already given the ***truth*** concerning General Reed's famous reply to the British commissioners, and I propose to follow it up with the publication of a few letters, interesting on account of the light which they shed upon our revolutionary history.

Many of the citizens of Philadelphia must remember Mrs. Sarah Kemp, who died in Race street, in 1820, at the advanced age of eighty-four years. Andrew Kemp, the only son of this respectable matron, entered the American army, almost at the very commencement of the struggle, and before, as his mother has often informed me, he had reached his majority. As he shall be my first witness against General Reed, it is proper to make the reader well acquainted with him. His gallantry, and a personal service which he had the good fortune to render to one of General Washingston's immediate staff, soon promoted him from the ranks, and he fought with great bravery, at the battles of White Plains, Trenton, Princeton, Brandywine, Germantown and Monmouth. Sergeant Kemp was one of the garrison of Fort Mercer, under the command of Colonel Greene, when that fortress was assailed in the autumn of 1777, by the Hessian troops, commanded by Colonel Donop. In this affair, which, though not one of the most remarkable, was one of the most brilliant of the Revolution, Sergeant Kemp particularly distinguished himself, and was wounded slightly in the arm, and severely in the left thigh by a musket ball: at the subsequent capture of Fort Mercer by Cornwallis, Kemp was one of the few who fell into the hands of the enemy--the remainder of the garrison succeeding in safely evacuating the fort. In a few weeks, he managed to effect his escape from Howe's winter quarters at Philadelphia, and immediately joined the American army at Valley Forge. The privations of that encampment, dreadfully aggravated the sufferings of poor Kemp; but, after languishing during the season in one of the military hospitals, he resumed active service in the spring, and served in May under Lafayette at the affair of Barren Hill. At the battle of Monmouth, he fought with his usual intrepidity, but the fatigues of the engagement renewed the affection of his imperfectly healed leg; and, about three weeks after, he was obliged to submit to its amputation. Upon leaving the army, he received from General Washington himself a certificate of conduct and character, which I copy from the original before me.

Head Quarters, June 23, 1778.

Sergeant Andrew Kemp is personally known to me as a brave and faithful soldier, who has served in several engagements, and who desires his discharge only in consequence of the loss of a limb, which unfits him for further service. His dutiful conduct is reported to me to be equal to his bravery; and he retires from the army with my good opinion and that of all whom I have heard speak of him.

(Signed,)   G. WASHINGTON.

From among other testimonials to Mr. Kemp's worth and conduct, which formed
to her dying day, the pride and solace of his aged mother, I select the following, given by Col. Samuel Smith, the late Mayor of Baltimore, and the gallant defender of Fort Mifflin against the six days' attacks of the British.

"Andrew Kemp has served with me three times; the last nearly four months. He was discharged from the army last month, in consequence of the loss of his leg and other bodily infirmities. I have always found his conduct exemplary. He came to me with high recommendations from officers whom he had previously served with, and fully realized what they had prepared me to expect from him.

(Signed,)   SAMUEL SMITH.
September 3, 1778."

This brave fellow fell a victim to his benevolent daring, during the prevalence of the yellow fever in this city, in 1798. Upon the death of his mother, the certificates of character which I have transcribed, and a number of his letters, of various dates, written while he was in the army, passed into the hands of the veteran, to whom in my former article, I referred, but whose name I am not *yet* at liberty to mention. From among them, I make two selections--the first a letter to his mother, who then resided in Chester County.

Camp, June 13th; 1788.

My Dear Mother,--You must be very uneasy not hearing from me so long, and the only wonder is that I am alive to give any account of myself. After my escape from Philadelphia, last November, I wrote to you, but whether you received my letter or not I cannot tell, for I have never heard a word of you since. We have had a dreadful time of it through the winter at Valley Forge. Sometimes for a week at a time with nothing but frozen potatoes, and even worse off still for clothing; sometimes the men obliged to sleep by turns for want of blankets to cover the whole, and the rest keeping watch by the fires. There is hardly a man whose feet have not been frost bitten. I have been laid by nearly the whole time on account of my leg, from which I suffered very much; and Doctor Le Brean insisted upon taking it off, but I would not suffer him; for which I have great reason to be joyful, for it is now nearly as well as ever, except a little stiffness, particularly after marching. But our distress from want of food and comfortable raiment, was nothing compared to the grumbling of some of the men, and I am sorry to say, of some of the officers. I really thought we should have a meeting once or twice; but we weathered through without it. Some hard things are said since about some of the officers, but the whole talk of the army is now about General Reed. There have been a good many attempts to conceal it from the men, but it has pretty much leaked out. This spring, it seems, King George sent over some Commissioners, as they call them, to endeavour to make a peace with us; and it turns out that General Reed has been in secret correspondence with them all the time, and was offered large amounts to play into their hands; but the bargain was broken off by his wanting more than they were willing to give. I know this much for certain; that one of their letters was taken to General Washington, and that the men were all called up at the dead of night, by beat of drum, and most of the officers called to Head Quarters. In the morning, General Reed was placed under guard, but released in about two hours. The letter was from one of the British Commissioners, in answer to one of his--he gave some explation, but it did not satisfy the General, but he was obliged to accept it, as the contrary could not be proved. I heard Captain Anderson tell Dr. Le Brean, that General

Washington was fully satisfied that Reed had been on the very point of betraying us all to the British, but that it could not be fully proved; and at such a time, it was better to keep a strict eye upon him, without getting the army into disgrace by exposure.

"Near the last of May, we had a smart little affair with the British at Barren Hill; it was the first time I was under marching orders since I left the hospital. The British army came very near surprising us after night--two of the sentinels of the picket guard having fallen asleep on their posts. But we managed to get across the river again with very little loss, only eight men killed and wounded, and three prisoners. I made a narrow escape, for I heard a bullet whistling by my ear as close as it could, without hitting. All well at home, I hope. Tell Sally not to forget to knit me a supply of woollen stockings, and a couple pair of mittens for next winter, for I dread the idea of another Valley Forge; and give her and Ann my kind love.

"From your affectionate son,
"ANDREW KEMP."

My object in giving this ***introductory*** letter is to show Mr. William B. Reed that the treachery of his grandfather was understood by the army at large, and that the knowledge of it was not confined to a few leading officers. ***Documents of a more precise, specific, and important character***, are in my possession, or within my means of access; and shall seasonably appear; but, unlike "***McDonough***," I do not choose to put my best foot foremost, and limp ever afterwards. I subjoin another letter from Sergeant Kemp, for the edification of Mr. Reed.

"Monmouth Court House, N. J., July 2d, 1778."

"Dear Mother,--I am laid up again, but after the fatigues of a great battle, and a great victory, which we fought on the 28th of June,--James Maris, who had his hand shattered by a bullet, has leave of absence for four weeks; and I drop a few lines by the opportunity which his going gives me. God be thanked, we have had a glorious victory! The British troops, commanded by Sir Henry Clinton, and ours by General Washington, were nearly matched--say ten thousand each. We fought from the forenoon till nigh dark; and our whole loss, killed and missing, is short of seventy, while the British lost about three hundred, and among them one Colonel Monks or Monkston. I have no great time for particulars. The men behaved very nobly; and the morning after, when we found that the British had decamped over night, the General [Washington,] thanked us all, from horseback. But one thing there is which has occasioned much disturbance among us. I mean the conduct of General Lee, who attempted to retreat, and who has since been put under order, to be court martialed.

"Then there's that General Reed has been behaving very strangely again. Not a man nor officer in the army that does not hate the sight of him; we all believe that he came very near betraying us, only that the General [Washington] found him out in time. We all remember Valley Forge last winter. Before the battle began, I myself heard Gen. Washington whisper to General Greene and Wayne, to keep a sharp eye upon Reed's movements, and if he made any suspicious attempt, to order him under arrest, and shoot him if he resisted. During the whole battle, I never saw him; but after the last gun was

fired, and when it was almost dark, General Reed suddenly made
his appearance from the rear, and gave out that he had just
had a horse shot in two under him, and asked for two men to go
and remove his saddle and holsters. I was one of them; we
examined the horse very carefully, and found him to be without
hurt or scratch; and he had plain enough died from mere heat,
which killed several horses and a number of men during the
day. The story has got wind--some laugh, but others shake
their heads about it. Jim Maris heard General Washington say
to General Wayne in the evening, that he abhorred the very
sight of Reed, and could never again put the least faith in
him. This is not the first time that General Reed has showed
the white feather. He pretended to have a horse killed under
him, in the same way at the Battle of Brandywine, and had two
men put in irons for talking about it. I am afraid my leg is
going to give me a good deal of trouble again It is very much
swollen, and discharges continually. They have me on the sick
list. My best love to Sarah and Ann.

"Your dutitful son,
(Signed)   "ANDREW KEMP."

Having given the testimony of Sergeant Kemp, I will now have the pleasure
of introducing to the notice of Mr. William B. Reed a letter from Col.
Samuel Smith, to his old friend in arms, Colonel ----, by whom I have been
so kindly supplied with much of the reminiscences which I have given to the
readers of the Journal, and who had addressed to Col. Smith a letter, the
nature and object of which will best be explained by the following reply:

"Senate Chamber, Washington, Feb. 15th, 1832.

"MY DEAR FRIEND,--Yours of the 9th was received yesterday, having been forwarded to me by my family from Baltimore, to which place you had addressed it, forgetting my still being in public life at Washington. I suppose you think that so old a man, and one who has led so busy and active a life, should take the evening of his days to his comfort and quiet reflection, and I am not sure but that you are right. Public life ought to have but little charms for either you or me; we have both seen enough of active service, and should devote the remnant of time which is left us, to settling our accounts with this world, and preparing for a better.

"I am gratified to hear of the task in which you tell me you are engaged. I do not know that it is in my power to afford you much of the assistance which you seem to think I can give; but such information as I can communicate is very cheerfully at your service. Upon my return to Baltimore, I will examine my papers; and whatever letters I can spare, which I may think likely to aid you in your labors, or illustrate the times of which you propose to write, shall be forwarded to your direction.

"I agree with you that many of the men, and not few of the events, of the Revolution, are very imperfectly understood. Take General Washington himself, for example: he is represented as having been cold and repulsive in his manner, when the very reverse was the fact. True, he was dignified and reserved, but always courteous, and, what I admired above all, always sincere. I never knew a man capable of stronger attachments; he had none of the vices of humanity, and fewer of its weaknesses than any man I ever knew. I do not believe Mr. Jefferson **meant** to be unjust; but the character drawn of

Washington, which appears in his recently published papers and correspondence, falls, in all respects, very far short of doing him justice. Mr. Jefferson had not the sort of mind which was entirely capable of appreciating, or even exactly understanding, a character like that of Washington's. I saw much of the old General in his latter days; visited him several times at Mount Vernon, and frequently at Washington. Doctor Craih, (my near connexion by marriage,) was long his physician and intimate friend, and was in attendance upon his death-bed. He has given me anecdotes innumerable of Washington's generosity and kindness of heart, which, though, not known to the world, ought to be. Of these, I will write to you more fully from home.

"I can communicate but little concerning Gen. Wayne, which you do not know already. His son, who lives somewhere in your state, I should take to be a proper person to whom to apply. I wish it were in my power to answer more fully than I can, your inquiries concerning General Reed. My personal acquaintance with him was limited. I shared in the deep dislike with which he was regarded, and his negotiations with the British commissioners, in the spring of 1778, made him obnoxious to the whole army, from the commander-in-chief to the lowest subaltern. You and I talked this matter over nearly fifty years since, and I have found nothing to change, but much to confirm, my opinions. It is a little too bad that this man should be reverenced by posterity as one of the purest of the men of the revolution, when you and I, and all who were really active in those times, know that nothing but accident prevented his taking the start of Benedict Arnold. Though not communicative, General Washington was always candid, and upon the subject of Reed's premeditated betrayal of the country to England, he has frequently conversed with me very freely. None

of the correspondence between Reed and the British
commissioners, fell into his hands except the letter from
Governor Johnston, and an enclosed note in cypher from Lord
Carlisle, but these contained sufficient to assure Washington
that a long correspondence had passed--that proposals had been
made and debated, and that Reed had finally submitted a
proposition which the commissioners were endeavouring to
reduce. With the explanation Reed gave you are familiar. No
one believed it, but it passed muster, for the only proofs
which *at the time* could be had, were the intercepted papers.
But ever after, Washington regarded Reed with great dislike,
and treated him with a manner strictly marked by the display
of his feelings. I was present when General Washington took
his final leave of his officers at New York, after the close
of the revolution, in the winter of 1783. The general's eyes
streamed with tears, he grasped each officer by the hand, but
when Reed approached him with extended hand, he started as if
bitten by a serpent, made a cold bow, and passed on.
Afterwards, at Annapolis, where Congress was then sitting, I
was present when General Reed was repeating to some half a
dozen of delegates, the old story of his refusal of the
commissioner's offer. Washington, who was within three yards
of him, turned away, and remarked to General Knox, "I know the
fellow well; he wanted but a price, and an opportunity, to
play us false as Arnold," and passed out of the room. There
was a general titter, and upon Reed's enquiring of General
Knox what it was that General W. had remarked, Knox replied,
"If you did not hear it, I advise you to follow the general,
and request him to repeat his observation." Reed was not a
fighting man. I do not say that he was a coward, but he was
always very careful of his person. His visit to England in
1784, I could never understand. His circumstances, just
before, were very much embarrassed, he had borrowed of all who

were willing to lend, and he paid nobody. Immediately upon his
return, he paid off all his debts, including one of three
thousand dollars to General Wayne, and commenced speculating
in real estate largly, when he was taken ill and died.

I have given you very near all I have concerning this person.
I have anecdotes from others, of which I will inform you
hereafter; as also, the particulars of several conversations
which I had with Washington respecting him. I have always,
from principle, been opposed to making mischief; but I have
always, at the same time, been opposed to trickery and
unfounded pretensions. Why the survivors of the Revolution
have so long permitted General Reed's treachery and baseness
to be glossed over, and himself converted into a patriot, is
to me a mystery; but the veil must be raised at last, and I
know of no one more capable of performing the task than
yourself.

"Let me hear often from you--and always be assured that I am
sincerely your friend,

SAMUEL SMITH.

I will close my budget of "documents" as "*McDonough*" would call them, for
the present. When I open it again, the information to be drawn forth will
be even more definite than that just given, and possibly, even still less
palatable to Mr. Reed. He will pardon me for troubling him with two
questions: Among the papers left by your grandfather, did you ever come
across a copy of a very remarkable correspondence had between that person
and General Anthony Wayne in 1781? If yea, why have you withheld it from
publication? Although *you* can answer this last question, I cannot; but I
will tell you, Mr. Reed, what I can do: I can lay my hands upon a copy of

the same correspondence, and I propose to entertain the readers of the Journal with a few selections, upon some not very distant occasion.

In Mr. Reed's selection of a ***period of time*** to be illustrated by the labors of "McDonough," it appears to me he has been unfortunate. If he had gone further back, he might have recounted some of the ***real*** exploits of his grandfather, and spared ***me*** the labor which his deficiencies have compelled me to undertake. If he had come a little further down, he might have dilated upon the performances of his father, a Recorder of the city of Philadelphia, and Treasurer and Secretary of the University of Pennsylvania. ***That*** labor, also, I fear, will devolve upon me.

VALLEY FORGE.

Monday, Sept. 25, 1842.

From the Evening Journal.

MR. WHITNEY--The communication of "McDonough" (alias U. S. Bank Reed,) in
this Morning's Court Chronicle, manifests that there is no small degree of fluttering among the wounded pigeons of the "Holy Alliance." The assumption of "McDonough" that ***you*** and "Valley Forge" are one and the same person, is a more novel than logical mode of disproving the truth of my allegations. But let Mr. Reed rest easy upon that score. ***Who*** I am, is very little to the purpose; ***what*** I assert is more germain to the matter--and let this lacquay of Nicholas Biddle deny ***that*** if he dare, or disprove it if he can. If my charges are ***true***, the identity of their author with the editor of the Evening Journal could not detract from their truth; if ***false***, a more obvious as well as conclusive mode of establishing their falsity presents itself.

But the truth is, that no arrow which has been shot into the camp of the "Holy Alliance" rankles more deeply, or has worked worse execution, than the exposure of the authorship of "McDonough." Not that Mr. Reed is by any means, either intellectually or extrinsically, the most formidable member of the combination; but now it is known that *he* is the author of those attacks upon the character of a good citizen, of a man against whom for years the minions of the Bank have been directing their warfare without the ability to discover a crevice in his coat of mail, the arm of the puny assailant falls paralyzed to his side, and his intended victim laughs at him in a tone of scorn, in which the whole community participates.

William B. Reed to prate of patriotism! *William B. Reed* to declaim upon honor and patriotism! For the chimney-sweep to prate of cleanliness would not be more anomalous. With what grace does the defence of the United States Bank come from this "McDonough" of the Chronicle, when we know him
to be the veriest lick-spittle that Nicholas Biddle, in his day of pride and power, ever retained in his service? As the friend of Nicholas Biddle, as his purchased tool and agent, rather, Mr. Reed has never, for an instant, hesitated to sacrifice to the promotion of the interests of the Bank, every public trust which for the time being was confided to his keeping. Why is it that Mr. Reed has never yet explained away or answered the very extraordinary and *specific* disclosures of *bribery* which a correspondent of the Ledger made against him in the summer of 1841? Disclosures so astonishing that the eyes of the public, although long accustomed to look upon the doings of the man with distrust, dilated with astonishment. He was accused by the correspondent of the Ledger with having as a member of the House of Representatives, *accepted bribes from the Bank of the United States*; the several amounts were specified; documents were even refered to; and yet Mr. Reed, instead of maintaining his good ground and confronting his accuser, flies the city, absents himself for some time upon the plea of a previously arranged excursion of pleasure; and

when, after his return, driven at length to a show of explanation, he parades in print an evasion of charges, so paltry that its sophistry would degrade the merest pettifoger in Mr. Biddle's Court of Criminal Sessions.

But since Mr. William B. Reed, alias Mr. U. S. B. McDonough, is so pure a patriot, and has such a holy horror of "treason" and "traitors," I will give him a few facts upon which to reflect, and with which he may enrich and illustrate his future lucubrations.

Fact No. 1.--That Mr. William B. Reed is, or claims to be, the grandson of General Joseph Reed, of Revolutionary memory.

Fact No. 2.--That Mr. William B. Reed is feelingly alive upon the subject of his grandfather's memory, and has devoted the labors of nearly his whole life to establish the popular delusion that his grandfather's patriotism underwent the severest test and ordeal of the revolutionary struggle.

Fact No. 3.--That Mr. William B. Reed has written essays, reviews and paragraphs innumerable, to induce the public to believe, that when in 1778 or 1779, Governor Johnstone and the other British Commissioners, proposed to General Reed a reward of 10,000 pounds sterling, and a lucrative office, upon condition that he would lend himself to the views of Great Britain, he indignantly spurned the proposal, and replied, "I am not worth the purchase, but such as I am, King George is not rich enough to make it."

Fact No. 4.--That no such proposal was ever made to General Joseph Reed, and that General Joseph Reed never made any such reply.

Fact No. 5.--That General Joseph Reed endeavoured to effect a negotiation with the British Commissioners, and actually commenced it, to ascertain what he might expect, in money and office, in case he succeeded in effecting a reconciliation between the colonies and the mother country, or in other words, that he would be instrumental in causing the revolted colonies to return to their allegiance to Great Britain!

Fact No. 6.--That General Joseph Reed, after much chaffering as to the price, finally proffered his services to the British Commissioners, to effect the objects mentioned in "Fact No. 5," for the sum of 10,000 pounds sterling in hand, a Chief Justiceship, and the right to a tract of land West and North-West of the then city of Philadelphia, upon a part of which the Cherry Hill Penitentiary is now erected, and the whole of which, is at this time probably worth from five to seven millions of dollars.

Fact No. 7.--That while this negotiation was pending, and while the hucksters were haggling as to the terms upon which it should close, it came to the ears of the American Commander-in-Chief, that General Reed was engaged in a very suspicious correspondence with the British Commissioners; that General Washington sent for General Reed, and in the presence of his staff, informed him of what he had heard, and demanded an explanation; and that General Reed, finding denial out of the question, admitted that overtures had been made to him by Governor Johnstone and his colleagues, but that he had replied to them; "I am not worth the purchase, but such as I am, King George is not rich enough to make it."

Fact No. 8.--That this patriotic reply of General Joseph Reed, to the attributed overtures of the British Commissioners, had its ***sole origin*** in the explanation with which he sought to dispel the suspicions of General Washington; that General Washington ever after continued to regard him with great distrust; and that several years subsequently, when General Reed, in the presence of General Washington, was descanting upon the patriotic reply with which he had foiled the British Commissioners, General Washington turned away in disgust, and remarked to a friend, in a tone of voice sufficiently audible to be heard by all present--***"I know the fellow well, and am satisfied that he wanted but a price and an opportunity to play us as false as Arnold."***

When Mr. Reed shall have sufficiently pondered over the facts thus enumerated, I shall descend the ladder a step from his grandfather, and come to his more immediate progenitor! Of him, I shall have the great question to ask--what is the reason of his aversion to sunshine, that he secludes himself all day like an owl or a bat? But the grandfather will suffice for the present. Mr. Reed has certainly taken uncommon pains to keep up the public delusion upon this subject. Let him know (what he will soon know to his mortification,) that there yet survives a veteran of the revolution--one whose mental faculties are undimmed by age--whose very physical frame, time has treated with tenderness and respect--whose keen and lively intelligence retains its ancient vigour--a Revolutionary soldier, who well knew Joseph Reed; who equally well knew George Washington; and who intends to give to the world, at no very distant day, his knowledge of them, and of much beside.

Mr. Reed has fair warning--let him look to it.

Monday, Sept. 19, 1842. VALLEY FORGE.

From the Evening Journal.

MR. WHITNEY:--Since your publication of my last, "McDonough" has slacked his fire wonderfully. It is surprising how one's tone becomes altered after the discovery is made that the former idea of *invulnerability* was a great mistake. The home truths pressed upon Mr. William Bradford Reed (I believe this is the first time that the public have been made acquainted with the learned gentleman's name in full) have proved to be of unpalatable flavor and difficult digestion; and it is not, therefore to be wondered at that they should have for him no relish. I have not yet done with the revolutionary reminiscences of his grandfather; that worthy whom "King George was not rich enough to buy," although, as he himself modestly admitted, he was "*not worth purchasing*:"

The writer of this paragraph had an opportunity, very many years since, when Mr. Reed was a student of the Pennsylvania University, of becoming somewhat intimately acquainted with his bent of mind; and if there ever was a school-boy despised and detested by his fellows, William was that youth. "The boy's the father of the man," and those who have known him only in his ripened years, if they apply the truth of this axiom, will have no difficulty in correctly conjecturing what must have been his early youth. Even then his predominant weakness was to almost daily, and by the hour, expatiate upon the merits of his *great* "grandfather," and to entertain boys, smaller and younger than himself, with the revolutionary exploits--more numerous and diversified far than those with a narration of which Othello beguiled the fair Desdemona, performed by that distinguished personage: and in particular, how "the General" had repulsed the proffered bribe of the Treasury of Great Britain, and his pick and choice of the most lucrative office in the Colonies.

Down to this day, this has continued to be the habit of Mr. Reed; and to such an extent has he indulged it, that he has become the butt and laughing stock of his acquaintance.

> "O, wad some Pow'r the giftie gie us
> To see oursels as others see us!
> It wad frae manie a blunder free us,
> An foolish notion!"

The extraordinary pains taken by Mr. Reed, to circulate the notion of his grandfather's more than Roman patriotism, would, of itself, be a circumstance calculated to induce suspicion of their being "something rotten in Denmark;" but, fortunately for the truth of history, the *proofs* of General Reed's treachery and meditated "treason," (if not *actual* treason, are extant--and the veteran, to whom in my last I referred, will, in due time, give them to the world. The descendants of General Reed have succeeded long enough in imposing upon the American people, as a patriot and a hero of the "times that tried men's souls," a wretch, who, in the emphatic language of General Washington, spoke in his presence and hearing, "wanted but a price and an opportunity to play us false as Arnold!" who, while his fellow soldiers were stinted of food and scant of clothing, was in actual treaty with the British Commissioners, to betray the American Army, and their Commander-in-Chief, and their cause, **and their Country**, to Great Britain, for the consideration of ten thousand pounds sterling, a judicial office, and a tract of land!!!

By a monstrous suppression of truth, and an adroit perversion of the explanation which General Reed gave to the demands of the American Commander-in-Chief, respecting his correspondence with the British Commissioners, his descendants have managed, so far, with tolerably general success, to thrust into the ranks of the Carrolls and Hancocks, the Putnams and Warrens of the Revolution, a "traitor," who entered into the struggle as a matter of speculation; and who, from the date of his appointment, in 1774, as one of the Committee of Correspondence of Philadelphia, down to the detection of the fact, some years after, that he was engaged in a correspondence with the British Commissioners, watched with untiring vigilance, for a proper "opportunity" to betray, for a sufficient "price," the cause, and the country, to the tender mercies of George the Third and his ministry! There is scarcely a Review or Magazine, published in the country, into which, under the pretext of reviewing some publication, Mr. William B. Reed has not contrived to obtrude some panegyric of his grandfather's patriotism--fulsome, even if true, but most monstrous when considered with reference to its unworthy object.

Not content with chaunting Gen. Reed's praise as an "invisible singer," Mr. Reed has not hesitated to take the field openly, and in person, and sound the trumpet in the ears and before the eyes of the astonished lookers on. Before every literary or collegiate association which he has been called on, or *finefied* to have himself invited to address, the eternal burden of his song has been, "I am the grandson of the great and good patriot, General Joseph Reed, of revolutionary memory, who replied to the emissaries of Great Britain, when they offered him his own terms to further the views of England, 'I am not worth the purchase, but poor as I am, King George is not rich enough to make it.'" At New York, a few years since--afterwards, in the Musical Fund Hall, in this city--more recently at Dickinson College--quite lately at Harvard University, in short, everywhere, and on all occasions, the self same tune has lulled his audiences into a general slumber. How any one whose cheek is not formed of brass, can stand up as Mr. Reed has accustomed himself to do, and thus dole out, on all occasions, and before all assemblies, the patriotism of a grandfather for whose "treason" he should blush, I am at a loss to imagine. Even if deserved modesty ought to insinuate that the tribute would be more appropriately paid, and in better taste, by other voices.

But the strongest part of all is, that Mr. Reed, with that full knowledge which I know him to possess (and which I will satisfy him that I *know* him to possess) of his grandfather's traitorous designs and conduct, should, nevertheless, have succeeded in steeling himself to the habit which has made him so supremely and universally ridiculous.

Whenever it is announced that a new work is in preparation, in any way connected with the events of the American Revolution, poor Mr. William B. Reed "gets the fidgets." He throws business, as Macbeth did physic,--to the dogs; he can hardly delay for the introduction of a supply of clean linen into his carpet-bag; but, jumping into the next steamboat or railroad car, he travels post-haste till he has reached the residence of the author, whom he never leaves till he has fully satisfied himself that the projected work is to contain nothing that can detract from the spurious fame of General Reed, or call into question the truth of his attributed reply to the British Commissioners. Poor Mr. Jared Sparks must have had a hard time of annoyance during the long series of years in which he was engaged in preparing for the press his editions of the correspondence of Washington

and Franklin. Mr. Bancroft, the author of *the* History of the United
States, is, at present, a particularly prominent object of Mr. Reed's
dread. Indefatigable in his researches he cannot have failed to become
possessed of some of the evidences of General Reed's "treason," and, stern
in his impartiality, it is not to be supposed that he will hesitate to
place before the world the character and doings of this miscreant in their
true colours. Fearful of this, Mr. Reed has long been engaged in playing
the *toady* to Mr. Bancroft: with what success thus far, remains to be
seen: but one thing is certain, that Mr. Bancroft will have placed in his
hands, in time to inform him fully for his preparation of that volume of
his history in which it will become necessary for him to introduce the name
of General Joseph Reed, letters and documents that will establish the
"treason" of that worthy beyond a doubt.

The last volume of Mr. Bancroft's work comes down no later than 1784; so
that there will probably appear another volume before the period of General
Reed's exploits will become the subject of his composition; and of this
length of time Mr. Reed will doubtless endeavor to take advantage and make
good use. He has just made a formidable demonstration upon Mr. Bancroft.
"At the recent literary festival at Cambridge," (to borrow the language of
Mr Reed, contained in his late letter to the editors of the National
Intelligencer, concerning Mr. Graham, the historian,) Mr. Reed's *toadying*
of Mr. Bancroft was the subject of general comment. Not content with the
display of his fulsome civilities on that occasion, Mr. Reed has since
forced an opportunity of volunteering to the editors of the National
Intelligencer, the letter to which I have just alluded; in which under the
pretext of honouring the memory of the late James Graham, Esq., the English
author of a History of American Colonies, Mr. Bancroft is plastered with
praise. It is thus that Mr. Reed seeks either to impose upon Mr. Bancroft
the same "Romance of American History," in which the grandfather is the
principal personage, with which he flatters himself he has duped every body
else, or to disarm him of any intention of publishing the *true* history of
his connection with the British Commissioners.--And what most of all

enhances the meanness of Mr. Reed's conduct is the fact, that, but a year or two since, he was accustomed, at the Whig political meetings of this city, to make Mr. Bancroft (who then held the office of Collector of the Port of Boston, and was a prominent Democrat,) the especial object of his abuse, lavished upon him in the most unmeasured terms.

Such is the man, who, with a thorough knowledge of his grandfather's delinquencies, persists in upholding him to the world as a true and sterling patriot; who, knowing him to be a "*Traitor*," steeped in "*Treason*" to the very eyelids, and seeking to barter away his country and its liberties for British gold and office, represents him, unblushingly, as the worthy compeer of Washington, a fellow labourer in the same vineyard, toiling from the rising to the setting of the sun!!! But Mr. Reed's race of eulogy of his ancestors is nearly run. The proof of that man's treachery, long known to the *few*, will soon be promulgated to the *many*--to the WORLD. How *then*, will Mr. William B. Reed feel, when he remembers his itinerant career of laudation; his journeyings by sea and by land, that the trumpet of General Joseph Reed's praises might be sounded? His essays, reviews, addresses, and heaven only knows what all besides? But, above all, how will he *then* feel when he remembers that, under the stolen name of a naval hero of the Late War, he, this worthy descendant of a Traitor and Tory of the Revolution, once devoted whole weeks to the malignant endeavour to fasten upon a pure and unoffending citizen the very crime of "Treason," of which he knew his own grandfather to have been guilty?

With one or two little anecdotes, (the character of which may somewhat surprise Mr. Reed at the extent and accuracy of my information,) I close for the present. I will select those which Mr. Reed has the best reasons for knowing to be true. During the visit of Lafayette to this country, the father of Mr. William B. Reed, (Mr. Joseph Reed, the late Recorder of Philadelphia,) called on the General at his quarters, in this city, and requested the honour of a private interview. The General (who had been waited upon by Mr. Reed before, in company with the authorities, and other citizens) intimated his numerous and pressing engagements; but Mr. Reed persisting, the interview was granted; one not strictly private, however, there being two other gentlemen present. Mr. Reed informed the General that his object was to obtain from him some revolutionary anecdotes, of which he was convinced he must possess a stock, of his father, the late General Joseph Reed. General Lafayette's countenance immediately fell: he endeavoured politely to evade Mr. Reed's request; at last, as Mr. Reed would take nothing short of downright refusal, the General was, at length, compelled to remark, "I am sorry to say, sir, that I am acquainted with no anecdotes of the late General Reed which it would be pleasant for his son or any of his friends to hear." Mr. R. having bowed himself out of the room in great confusion, the General remarked to one of the gentleman present, in surprise, "This is very strange! Can it be possible that Mr. Reed is ignorant of the opinion which the officers of the Revolution entertained of his father?" And now for another, in which Mr. William B. Reed himself figured. A year or two before the death of Bishop White, he called on the venerable prelate and made a request precisely similar to that with which his father had troubled General Lafayette. Anxious to spare his feelings, the good Bishop endeavoured to change the subject; but, no other mode offering of escaping from the pertinacity of Mr. Reed, he said to him, "Young man, upon the subject of your grandfather, the least that's said, will be soonest mended!"

In my next, I will so far follow the example of McDonough, as to publish a few "Documents," the original of which will be consigned, before long, to Mr. Bancroft.

VALLEY FORGE.

Sept. 23d, 1842.

From the Evening Journal,

MR. WHITNEY:--The Jeremiads of the Forum and the Evening Courier shall not

deter me from the task which I have deliberately assumed, and which I mean to carry out, of exposing the treachery of the late General Joseph Reed, and the delinquencies of his living grandson, Mr. William Bradford Reed. Why, instead of ***deprecation***, do not these journals give ***disproof***? Is a fellow to be canonized as a saint, because he is no longer of the living? Then let all history be rewritten, and let the puling mawkishness which the hypocrites call manly indignation, reject from the page of history the infamy of a Nero, the cruelty of a Tiberius, and the treason of an Arnold. If it be proper for the entertainment or instruction of posterity, that the vices and crimes of the men of history shall be faithfully detailed, why should not the "***treason***" of General Reed, contemplated or effected, be spread upon his country's annals? Above all, when he and his descendants have adroitly disguised his villainy with the varnish of incorruptible patriotism, why should the hand which has the power to tear off the mask, and expose the enormity of guilt, be made to fall, self-withheld and self-paralyzed, from the effort? These are questions which admit of but one reply. I shall ***go on***, and in continuation of my developments, I here subjoin another letter from Col. Samuel Smith to the same gentleman to whom was addressed his last.

Baltimore, October 2d, 1832.

MY DEAR COLONEL--I acknowledge the receipt of your two very kind letters since I left Washington, and thank you for the acceptable accompaniment of the last. Also, for the pamphlet on Cholera which you have sent--I loaned it to several of our medical gentlemen, and they all seem to think highly of it. Our people have been much alarmed, and I think with good reason. For my own part, I entertain but little uneasiness. I

have lived a long life, and though I am far from tired of it,
I am ready to go whenever it pleases him who gave it to take
it away.

Looking over my paper, I have directed copies to be made up
such as seem adapted to your purpose. These, and some
original, I will send to your direction, whenever I hear from
you again, and you inform me how to send them. I have but few
letters from Gen. Washington--the ***originals*** I cannot consent
to part with; but copies are cheerfully at your service. I
have had a copy taken of a very remarkable correspondence
between General Wayne and General Reed, which awaits your
directions. I was on a visit to Wayne shortly after its close;
he read it to me, and I was so much struck with it, that I
requested leave to take a copy, which he gave me. You will
find it a curiosity, and it is another development of the real
character of Reed. I think I formerly mentioned I knew but
little of Gen. Wayne, with which you are not already
acquainted, and I may say much the same as to Putnam, except
what I had from conversation with General Washington. I have
never been able to make up my mind how far Gen. Gates was
concerned in the movement for his promotion, at Washington's
expense. He certainly did not openly encourage it. It is so
delicate a matter, I did not like to directly question General
Washington. Once or twice, in conversation, I thought he was
coming to the point, but he broke off without reaching it.
Many of Conway's movements against Washington had a tact and
address about them, for which Gates generally received the
credit. Towards the close, his calumnies of Washington were
disgustingly obscene--I mean Conway's. General Reed was well
known to be deeply engaged in this conspiracy. But he lacked
the courage of Conway, and was wholly without the rashness
which so frequently marked the latter. Reed was a cautious and

cunning plotter--he never looked one in the eye. Lee, who
mortally hated him, had a common saying, "that Reed's face was
stamped with the devil's favorite brand." I was once present
when he made the remark in the presence of Reed, without
observing him. Reed stepped forward, and angrily demanded
"what was that, sir?" Lee bowed and repeated the observation,
amid roars of laughter from all present. General Reed left the
spot, remarking, "you shall hear from me shortly;" to which
Lee replied, "I doubt that." Nothing further ever came of it.

Conway and Reed were decidedly the two most unpopular men in
the army--with this difference, that Conway, though disliked,
was respected, until his calumnies of Washington were carried
to their extent. Of Conway's duel with General Cadwalader I
have no particulars which you do not possess. Conway became
nearly involved in another duel on Reed's account. He took up
a quarrel of Reed's but it was compromised. Reed was publicly
insulted, and submitted like a boarding-school miss. My
sentiments on some subjects have changed with my advancing
years; but I well remember the surprise which I felt, and
which the whole army expressed, that a soldier, and one
wearing epaulettes, should patiently submit to the epithet of
"liar," and a threat of having his nose pulled. It may have
been a conscientious scruple; but he did not hesitate to get
others into difficulties.

In 1783 or '84, I had business which called me to Alexandria.
To my delight, I met General Washington there, and he insisted
upon my accompanying him home. The weather was wet and cold,
and, for a wonder, as he expressed himself, he was without
visiters but me. I remained at Mount Vernon several days and
had many and long conversations with the General. While there,
one of his newspapers mentioned the return of General Reed

from England, in feeble health; and this induced a
conversation concerning that person. I reminded the General of
the coolness with which I had seen him treat Reed at the final
leave-taking of his officers; and of the remark I had
afterwards heard him make at Annapolis. The particulars I gave
you in my letter from the Senate. General Washington rose,
stamped his foot somewhat violently; then instantly checking
himself, he paced the room slowly, speaking while he walked. I
remember every thing he said as plainly as if it had been
spoken only yesterday. He stated to me, that he had no doubt
that General Reed had long been in treaty with the British
before the arrival of their Commissioners in Philadelphia in
1778; and that, after the treaty of peace, in 1783, he
received information, which placed it beyond question, that,
in the appointment of the Commissioners, the British Ministry
had selected Lord Carlisle with express reference to an
acquaintance which he had had with Reed, when Reed was in
England, seventeen or eighteen years before.

He mentioned that, in 1777, while the army was yet encamped at
Valley Forge, Mrs. ----, a lady from Philadelphia, with whom
Reed was long known to have had a criminal intercourse, was
arrested within the lines, and that her suspicious conduct
induced a search, which led to the discovery of a letter upon
her person, from Governor Johnstone to General Reed, and
enclosing a note from Lord Carlisle, which was in *cypher*.
This letter related to overtures upon which Donop, the Hessian
officer, and General Reed, had already exchanged their views;
pronounced them to be somewhat extravagant; and suggested that
Reed had better close the arrangement which had been proposed
to Count Donop, and he would have no reason to complain. The
ten thousand pounds of which Donop spoke, Johnstone said would
be immediately paid, and he did not think there would be any

difficulty about the land or its equivalent; but of the
office that Donop mentioned, he (Governor Johnstone,) could
not speak with confidence; upon that subject, the enclosed
note from Lord Carlisle, Governor Johnstone said, would inform
General Reed more definitely. This note being in cypher,
General Washington informed me he never succeeded in having
unravelled. Immediately upon receiving these papers, General
Washington informed me he called a council, and sent for Reed.
He placed the two letters in General Reed's hands, and
demanded an explanation. Unfortunately, the officer whom he
had sent for Reed had informed him what had happened and he
had thus some time and opportunity for preparation. Reed
professed himself unable to read the note in cypher, and said
he did not know what it meant.

As to the letter from Governor Johnstone, he explained that
overtures had been some time before made to him, offering him
his own reward, upon condition of his bringing about a peace,
but that he had replied, "that he was not worth the purchase,
but poor as he was, King George was not rich enough to make
it." When General Washington demanded why he had not before
informed him of this communication, Reed replied, that though
he was incorruptible, he was afraid of letting it be known
what offers had been made, lest other officers might have been
tempted to accept them. Reed was placed under arrest until
further inquiries were made, but they were not successful, and
he was released. The female upon whom the letters were
detected, had been released, after being searched, and though
every effort was made to get her again it was fruitless.
General Washington added, that through the rest of the war, he
watched Reed narrowly, and trusted him with nothing; and
though he had no further *proof* of his guilt, he was
satisfied that his treason had existed. But General Washington

informed me, that ***after the peace***, he had received information, the source of which he was not at liberty to divulge, but the truth of which he had satisfied himself of, that nothing but the accidental intercepting of Johnstone's and Carlisle's letters, had prevented Reed's consummation of treason. He had become fully convinced, after the disbanding of the army, that Reed had had numerous personal interviews during the war, with leading British officers; that he had seen Donop at Burlington; that he had been repeatedly within the British lines, and that he ***now*** knew that, after the battle of Germantown, he had visited the English General, Howe, at his Head Quarters, in Philadelphia.

I have now given you, accurately, the substance of General Washington's conversations upon this subject. It fully accounts for his marked treatment of Reed at New York and Annapolis; and it must convince you what a precious rogue in grain this counterfeit patriot was.

My letter will not reach you for some time after its date. My arm is stiff, and I write slowly; and, although I have but one date, I have written a little each day for four days. God bless you, my old friend, and make me hear frequently from you.

Yours very truly,
SAMUEL SMITH.

I allow Mr. William Bradford Reed till Saturday to meditate upon this epistle. On that day, unless ***he*** should anticipate me, and publish the correspondence with Wayne, to which Colonel Smith refers, ***I*** shall have

the pleasure of presenting it to the public eye. It is a light that ought
not to be hidden under a bushel; but should be placed upon an elevation
high as the summit of the Bunker Hill Monument, that it may be seen far and
wide.

VALLEY FORGE.

October 1st, 1842.

October 5th, 1842.

MR. WHITNEY.--While exposing the demerits of Mr. William Bradford Reed,
I
have no disposition to disparage whatever of ability or information he may
really possess; and concerning the letter, I cheerfully acknowledge that he
has made himself very thoroughly acquainted with the true character of the
leading men and events of the American Revolution.

But it is ***this*** that constitutes his chief shame. In his absurd panegyrics
of his "Grandfather," he has not been imposed upon; he is seeking to impose
upon others, and in this he has, to a very considerable extent, succeeded;
he is sinning against the excess of light and the superfluity of knowledge.
Possessing the most ample proofs of his grandfather's treachery to his
country in the darkest hour of his country's peril, Mr. William B. Reed has
not hesitated to hold him up to that very country which he sought to
betray, and ***did*** well nigh betray, and ***would*** have betrayed, but for the
timely interception of his treasonable correspondence with the British
Commissioners, as one of the most glorious and incorruptible of the
patriots who fought and suffered for the establishment of American
Independence! The guilt of this will cling to Mr. Reed enduringly.

Never can he shake off its contamination. Could he escape from the odium of his more immediate personal delinquencies; his fawning sycophancy of Nicholas Biddle; his dirty work in behalf of that man for money, not for love; could he deluge with Lethean ocean the public memory, his malpractices as attorney-general; his venal career as a member of the Legislature; could he induce the public to overlook the bribes which he pocketed under the pretext of *fees* received for services never performed--bribes, the amount of which and the dates of whose reception, are well known, and sustainable by documentary reference;--could all this be erased, as systematic and persevering labours, from his boyhood upward, to delude a much injured country into reverence for the memory, not of the contemporary, but of the ***predecessor*** of Benedict Arnold in "treason" have won for him an infamy from the consequences of which escape is impossible.

I have heretofore referred, in general terms, to Mr. Reed's numerous applications, by writing and in person, to such survivors of the Revolution, or their descendants, as he supposed could furnish the information he desired, for anecdotes of General Reed; a part of my labours, hereafter to be entered upon, will be to narrate not a few of the rebuffs and rebukes this unfortunate Doctor Syntax in search of the biographical Pickenesque has experienced, and the minute fidelity with which my sketches shall be marked, will contribute, let me assure Mr. Reed, no less to his surprise than mortification, nay, I will establish that much of the information, that many of the documents, which *I* propose to lay before the readers of the Evening Journal, *he* and his brother, the Professor, possess; that copies of some of the latter have long been in their hands; and that Mr. William B. Reed has solicited the transfer or destruction of the originals. But I will even do more than all this, I will, in at least two instances, ***publish his own letter***, praying for the loan if not the gift, of original papers affecting the fame of his grandfather. ***Even here*** I do not mean to stop. I shall show that Mr. Reed succeeded in inveigling from the possession of a gentleman of my acquaintance, for a pretended temporary purpose, a letter, the publication of which he supposed; and a part, I may say a prominent part, of Mr. Reed's scheme to perpetuate the delusion of his grandfather's patriotism, has been to write or call upon, every person projecting any work connected with the Revolution; and by tendering information, or otherwise volunteering his assistance, to deceive or disarm. He has played his game, so far, with very clever success; and, as I formerly mentioned, it is one which he is at present engaged in practising upon Mr. Bancroft--that same Mr. George Bancroft, whom, at a political meeting in this city, held some four or five years since, he so delicately described as a "tin cannister tied to the tail of Martin Van Buren, while Martin Van Buren, was running through the street, like a hot slut, with the whole kennel of loco-focoism bawling at her heels!" Adapting this figure to circumstances, as it might be introduced with great effect, into Mr. Reed's collegiate eulogy upon the services and patriotism of his grandfather.

In Col. Smith's last published letter to Col. ----, he promised to furnish the latter with copies of certain letters, and in another he says.

> "I cannot answer your inquiry about Captain Anderson. I knew several officers of that name, but can recal nothing particular concerning any of them. I once received a letter from a person some where in the State of Delaware, calling himself Henry Anderson, inquiring about his uncle Captain Anderson, of the Revolutionary army, but I have not retained, or mislaid the letter, and cannot call to mind his more particular address. But even this defective information may serve to put you on the scent.

> "Your son will tell you much for me that I would otherwise write. My rheumatism has prevented my showing him as much of the civilities of our town as I would have liked, but you will excuse me.

> "Most truly and sincerely,

"your old friend,
"SAMUEL SMITH.

From among the accompaniments of this letter transmitted by Col. Smith, I select, for incorporation in the present article, the following correspondence between General Anthony Wayne and General Joseph Reed. The
"*Numbers*" with which they are prefixed appear to be of General Wayne's own addition.

No. 1.

GEN. A. WAYNE,

My Dear General--

Only the day before yesterday I heard of your being here, and then but by accident, or I should have addressed you upon the subject of this communication. For several months there has been a rumor industriously circulated in this city, that during the last summer, you stated while in "South Carolina," in the presence of General Greene and other officers, that my conduct at the battles of Brandywine and Monmouth had subjected me to the imputation of timidity. It is added that you referred disparagingly to circumstances which occurred at *Valley Forge*, and revived the exploded calumny, for the truth of which you personally vouched, that I had signified my acceptance of the terms then offered me by the Commissioners, which you know that I spurned with scorn.

Of course you will understand me to be satisfied that you never did use any language of the kind, but, as these remarks have been propogated by persons who, I have every reason to believe, are no less your enemies than mine. I am anxious to afford you an opportunity for their contradiction, and this I have to request you will promptly give me.

I should be sorry that malicious and designing persons should have it in their power to disturb the harmony of the relations which I have so long enjoyed with one upon whose friendship I set so high a value, and for whom I entertain a peculiar esteem.

With great respect and cordiality,
I am my Dear General, yours, &c.,
JOS. REED

Dec'r 26th, 1783.

No. 2.

Philadelphia, December 27th, 1783.

Sir--The cool effrontery of your note yesterday surprised me. By what right you presume to refer to any harmony of relations between us, and to speak of the value of my "friendship" I am at a loss to comprehend. That harmony was first disturbed by the pecuniary difficulties in which you so dishonestly involved me, and from which I am only now beginning to extricate myself, apart from which I could entertain no feelings of "friendship" for an officer for whom I have such abundance of reasons for entertaining sentiments of a very different description. I have no doubt that my remarks to General Greene and others have been correctly reported to you, not only in South Carolina and Georgia, but years ago in Pennsylvania, and within the immediate reach of your personal demand. I have never hesitated, on all proper occasions to express myself in similar terms. I never merely intimated that your conduct at the battles of Brandywine and Monmouth had subjected you "to the imputations of timidity," but I have always said that your behaviour at those battles, particularly that of Chad's Ford, should have secured your dismissal from the army.

What you refer to as "the exploded calumny" of your negotiations with the enemy at Valley Forge, I in common with every officer in the army, with whom I have ever conversed upon the subject, including the Commander-in-chief, believe to be strictly well-founded.

I am Sir, yours,
ANTHONY WAYNE.

To Joseph Reed.

VALLEY FORGE.

We take the following communication of Mr. Smith, from the North American of this morning.

"In compliance with this arrangement, I came to this city this evening, accompanied by three of my friends conversant with my father's handwriting, viz; Hon. Louis McLane, Robert Gilmore, and Robert Purviance, Esqrs., and was met at the place and hour of appointment by William B. Reed and Henry Reed, Esqrs., and waited there until half-past eight o'clock, without the appearance of the author of "Valley Forge," or any of his friends.

JNO. SPEAR SMITH.

Washington House, Parlor No. 3,

Monday, October 24th, 1842.

In relation to this matter, we received through the Post-Office this morning, the following explanation from Valley Forge.

"Mr. WHITNEY:--I am unable to express my mortification at the unhappy and unexpected accident which has prevented my meeting the Messrs. Reed and Mr. John Spear Smith this evening, at the time and place appointed by them, for the purpose of having tested the authenticity of General Samuel Smith's letters to Colonel ----, Col. ---- is my near relative, and though in his ninety-third year, has till last Thursday, enjoyed the most excellent health for one of so advanced an age. As he will not permit the originals to be taken out his sight, I intended of course that he should accompany me as one of my three friends. His sudden and severe illness has rendered this impossible; he refuses to part with the documents even for a temporary purpose, and I have thus been compelled to submit for the present to this most mortifying piece of ill-fortune.

No doubt the exultation of the Messrs. Reed will be violent,

but let me say to them, it will be but short-lived. But a
brief time will pass, and all the papers which I have
published, and many more which are yet to come, will be fully
proved and laid before the public. When Colonel ----'s health
is restored, I do not doubt that I shall prevail upon him to
place them in my hands, when I shall see Mr. John Spear Smith
with them at Baltimore and have the Messrs. Reed see them
here.

VALLEY FORGE.

October 24th, 1842."

We do not approve of this course of procedure on the part of Valley Forge,
nor do we think it a proper one. We think he ought to have met Mr. Smith
and the Messrs. Reed at the place and time appointed, and made the
explanation in person. Under any circumstances, we think it was due to them
as well as to ourselves. The proposition which was made by Valley Forge
having been accepted by the above-named gentlemen, what reason can there
be
for longer preserving his incognito? Indeed he expressed his willingness,
in one of his notes, which we publish below, to unveil himself as soon as
the proposition he made was accepted.

We had, from the first, as we have now, the fullest confidence that the
letters purporting to be from the late General S. Smith were genuine, as
well as that the intentions of Valley Forge, so far as concerned ourselves,
were fair, and that he would establish the authenticity of those letters,
and the other documents contained in his communications.

Our belief in the genuineness of the letters of General Smith, was
strengthened by the perusal of a letter which we now have before us,

addressed to General Joseph Reed, by General John Cadwalader, in 1783, which corroborates what those letters contain. In that letter the latter gentleman says, "Having fully stated the temper of men's minds at this alarming period, and the situation of public affairs, I shall now recite the conversation and circumstances relating thereto, which I have avowed in my letter to you of the 10th September, as having passed between us at Bristol.

"I had occasion to speak with you, a few days before the intended attack on the 20th December, 1776, and requested you to retire with me to a private room at my quarters; the business related to intelligence--a general conversation, however, soon took place concerning the state of public affairs, and after running over a number of topics, in an agony of mind, and despair strongly expressed on your countenance, and tone of voice, you spoke your apprehensions concerning the event of the contest; that our affairs looked very desperate, and we were only making a sacrifice of ourselves; that the time Gen. Howe's offering pardon and protection to persons who should come in before the 1st January, 1777, was nearly expired; and that Galloway, the Allens, and others, had gone over and availed themselves of that pardon and protection offered by said proclamation; that you had a family, and ought to take care of them, and that you did not understand following the wretched remains (or remnants) of a broken army; that your brother (then Colonel or Lieutenant Colonel of the militia--but you say of the five month's men, which is not material) was then at Burlington with his family, and that you had ordered him to remain there, and if the enemy took possession of the town, to take a protection and swear allegiance--and in so doing he would be perfectly justifiable.

"This was the substance, and I think nearly the very words; but that, "you did not understand following the wretched remains (or remnants) of a broken army*! I perfectly remember to be the* very words!"

The letter of General Cadwalader contains the letters of P. Dickinson, John

Nixon, Benjamin Rush, David Lenox, A. Hamilton, and a numbers of other persons, confirming what we have quoted.

The subjoined notes from Valley Forge gave us confidence in the fairness of his intentions.

> R. M. WHITNEY, Esq: Dear Sir--I observe an invitation in yesterday's Journal, for me to call at, or send to, your office, for some information which you have to impart. For reasons which I shall have the pleasure of expressing to you hereafter in person, I am anxious to preserve my *incognito*, for the present, even with my nearest friends; and this consideration will prevent my *calling*. I am also at a loss to know how to *send*; but if you will drop me a few lines in the letter box of the Post-office, I shall not fail to receive them.
>
> Very truly, &c.,
> VALLEY FORGE.
> *September 23d, 1842.*
>
> Please direct to "Ambrose Anderson, Philadelphia."
>
> R. M. WHITNEY, Esq., Dear Sir,--I am favored with your note, refering me to General Cadwalader's pamphlet, which you inform me has been abstracted from the Philadelphia Library. I have access to *material*, far beyond any thing in importance and value which could possibly be obtained by General Cadwalader; nevertheless the *abstraction* of his pamphlet is a circumstance which I will not fail to turn to good account. The gentleman to which I so often refer, in my communications as the revolutionary soldier who has furnished me with information, is a near relative of mine, who knew Gen. Joseph

Reed thoroughly. I shall continue my communications from time to time; and you may rely upon my giving you nothing, which does not admit of literal substantiation. Among other letters which I have, are several from "George Clymer," (whom you mention in your note,) which hit the nail on the head.

Will you permit me the liberty of suggesting a continuance of your vigorous editorials upon Stephen Girard? The word "finessed" in my last, your compositor has transformed into *finified*.

Respectfully &c.,
VALLEY FORGE.
Sept. 25, 1842.

REUBEN M. WHITNEY, Esq., Dear Sir,--I am afraid that, in copying Sergt. Kemp's first letter, I have made an error of date, on which account I am glad my communication has not appeared to-day, as it gives me an opportunity of correction. I am anxious to avoid even the slightest mistake in my communications. The letter is dated "June 23rd, 1778." I am not certain that I did not so transcribe it; but if I did not, be good enough to make the correction. I particularly wish you would *italicise* my interrogatory to Reed relative to his grandfather's correspondence with General Wayne. There is a *point* in it which *he* will fully understand, and which will give him more uneasiness than all else. I intend reserving my extracts from that correspondence for the very last.

Respectfully, &c.
VALLEY FORGE.
Sept. 27, 1842.

R. M. WHITNEY, Esq.,--Dear Sir--I am provoked to find that, upon comparing my copy of Col. Smith's letter to Col. ----, with the original, that I have made another error! I hope this will reach you in time for its correction. Speaking of his visit to Gen. Washington at Mount Vernon and ***Washington***, it should be, and ***Philadelphia***.

Respectfully, &c.,
VALLEY FORGE.
Sept. 28, 1842.

R. M. WHITNEY,--Dear Sir--I have been absent for a day or two from the city, and did not receive your note until to-day. I enclose a note for publication--oblige me by letting it appear to-morrow. I cannot imagine how so stupid an error could have occured as the erroneous date of Kemp's discharge by Gen. Washington. But the error almost corrects itself--as Kemp's letter of July 2d, speaks of the battle of Monmouth on the 28th. I do not know whether the blunder is that of your workman, or mine in the haste of transcribing. One or two other errors, which are mine, I made the subject of two notes, which I addressed you through the Post-office. My absence from town, and my intended absence to-morrow, prevent my preparing another article for Saturday. Possibly, I will have it ready for Monday, and certainly for Tuesday. Acknowledge its receipt, and that it will appear on Monday or Tuesday. I have not yet come to the ***real gems*** of my budget. Reed shall have a surfeit.

Respectfully, &c.,
VALLEY FORGE
Sept. 30, 1842.

R. M. WHITNEY, Esq: Dear Sir--Nothing could have afforded me more pleasure than the publication which has been made by the Reeds. It has given me the opportunity, which I have from the first been seeking, of bringing the question of General Reed's revolutionary exploits to a *crisis*. I pledge myself to you, that I will overwhelm them with confusion and shame.

I have not called for your letter at the Post-office, because *I know that I am watched*; and I do not desire to be known till the adoption of my proposition to the Reeds, of which I speak in the accompanying communication, and which I will furnish for publication in Monday's Journal. They have fallen completely into the snare.

Yours, &c., very truly,
VALLEY FORGE.
October 14, 1842.

In his explanatory communication of yesterday's date, Valley Forge speaks of many more papers "which are yet to come:" we suppose he means yet to be published. If so, we feel constrained to say now, that we cannot publish any thing more relating to the matter until he announces to us, at least, his real name.

From the Evening Journal.

R. M. WHITNEY, Esq: Dear Sir,--I am pained beyond measure, at the situation in which I have been so unfortunately instrumental in placing you. But for circumstances *which I cannot possibly control*, I would promptly communicate to you my name and residence. A pledge, rigidly exacted by my venerable relative, Col. ----, and solemnly given by me at the time he consented that I should communicate to you the letters of the late General Smith, and the other papers with which he furnished me, that I should not make either him or myself known without his consent, binds me as with links of iron. Col. ---- is slowly recovering from the paralytic affection with which he was seized on the 20th of this month; and let me assure you, most sacredly and solemnly, that as soon as his health is sufficiently restored to allow a conversation of any length to be had with him, I will not fail to convince him of the propriety--of the *necessity*--of permitting me to call upon you, or invite you to his residence, where, preliminary to my taking the proper steps to convince the public of their authenticity, I may exhibit to you all the writings which have been so exultingly prounounced to be "audacious forgeries."

You do me but justice, when you say, that "a careful perusal of the letters of Valley Forge, confirms the belief, that he is neither an impostor nor a forger of letters." Why should I be? What motive could induce any rational being to originate a *fabrication* so sure to be detected? You will find, ere very long, that I have given you nothing but the truth. Only *one* liberty did I venture to take with any of the correspondence--that was from considerations of delicacy, which I now believe to have been *fastidious*, and to which, at the time, I reluctantly yielded. In Gen. Smith's letter to Col. ----, dated Oct. 2d, 1832, I substituted a *blank* for the name of *Mrs. Ferguson*," which Gen. Smith gives as that of the lady from whom was taken the letter of Governor Jonstone to Gen. Reed. This, the *only* alteration I ever made, you must allow, was a pardonable error.

"Truth is mighty and must prevail;" and in this case, to the joy of your friends, and the consternation of your enemies, it shall be signally exemplified. *For the present*, let me entreat you to rest satisfied with my assurances; assurances which will soon be most thoroughly redeemed; and that you will desist from your endeavor to discover who I am--efforts which can give you but vain trouble, which *must* prove fruitless; for the precautions which I have adopted for the preservation of my *incognito*, it is impossible to overcome.

Very truly, &c.,
VALLEY FORGE.

October 29th, 1842.

From the Evening Journal, October 31st.

"Valley Forge" and General Joseph Reed--Is there a Sepulchral Sanctuary for Public Men?--The success of the American Revolution--Justice and Truth essential Elements of History--"Forgery"--The Editor, &c.

Whatever motives may have actuated "Valley Forge" to the publication of documents affecting the revolutionary services and fame of General Joseph Reed, and we pretend not either to scan them, or doubt their honorable complexion--for truth, when on the side of country and patriotism, admits not of suspicion or mistrust--whatever motive, we say, may have impelled him to the revelation of these important historical documents, there can exist no doubt as it respects the principle which sustains the ransacking of the grave, for the sake of *truth*. Begin at any period of history, however early, and it will be found that *public men* have always been considered as public property--their characters, their conduct and their opinions, belonging to the world, with no privilege of sanctuary, either in life or in the *tomb*. It was so with the Hebrews, it was so with Persians, the Babylonians, the Grecians, the Romans, the French, the English, and even the Chinese. Indeed, so obvious is the principle, as almost to dispense with argument. It bears on its very face, the irresistible force of a first principle; for if the grave cannot cover up the *good* deeds of men, it never can be made to conceal their evil ones. The lessons of history, like the lessons of life, are derived more from the wicked than the good. The striking contrast of example, comes from the man who has perpetuated deeds that curdle the blood with fear, or crimson the cheeks with shame. Virtue is negative, quiet, undismayed--but vice rides aloft on the back of desecrated principles and violated laws, accompanied by the tumultuous rush of a moral whirlwind, overturning the fruits, blossoms and harvest of life; bearing blasts upon its brow, and leaving havoc in its train. And so do the laws of all well governed countries dispose of the remains of notorious felons, who, instead of being suffered to repose in the grave, are denied all interment; their bodies being delivered over to the surgeons for the benefit of science, or exposed on a gibbet, till the crows, eagles and vultures, devour their flesh, and then, even their bones are left to blacken in the winter's blast, as a warning to man, to shun the deeds that led them to their doom.

Where is the sepulchral sanctuary for Buonaparte? or for Nero? or for Marius, Sylla, Otho, Galba, Charles of Burgundy, or Ferdinand of Spain? How many patriots are commemorated in the Lives of Plutarch? Expunge from the History of England the great scoundrels who disgraced their diadems, on the plea of sepulchral sanctuary, and how many kings will remain to grace their pages with the splendor of their virtues? The same question may be asked in reference to all histories, and the same answers given; there would be no history, if the grave silenced the tongue to speak of the vices and crimes of the dead who disgraced their nature.

To return to the principle of success, as a standard of virtue, in great revolutionary movements. The intrinsic merit of a civil movement, or commotion, to produce a change of government by force of arms, or social intimidation without bloodshed, is not sufficient to glorify its actors. Success is essential to give renown which confers fame and glory on its authors. This was fully understood during the American Revolution. A host of calculating spirits stood mute, inactive, or luke-warm, watching the changes of the contest, and fearful of embarking in a cause that might miscarry. In such a crisis, the wavering, the doubtful and the timid, were more dangerous to their country's cause than the open traitor in arms against freedom. The generous, the brave, the frank, the self-devoted patriot, rushed headlong into the contest, putting in peril, life, honor, property, fame, family, friends, children--all that is dear to life, and all that life endears. The calculating and timid palsied their daring counsels by weak irresolution of wicked duplicity. Among these time-servers, it seems General Joseph Reed stood prominent. Careful of his person, he shunned danger. Calculating the probable miscarriage of the Revolution, he occupied the prudent ground of a tory royalist, seeming to battle for liberty, but ready, at any moment; to assume the scarlet uniform, and shout "God save King George!" A traitor in his heart to the cause of Independence, lest that cause, by failing, should make him a traitor to his king, for whom he felt a warmer affection than for the rebels--he stood always on the alert, to join the British, or to appear their greatest foe; practising the meanest arts to seem brave, yet always held in open contempt for his timidity and cowardice. If the Revolution succeeded, he calculated to pass for a patriot. If the royal arms triumphed, he stood prepared to claim the rewards of his fidelity to the KING, more valuable than an open adherent because a secret spy, who betrayed the cause of the rebels, while pretending to fight under its colors, in the uniform of an American Officer of the army of George Washington!

Such appears to have been the character of General Joseph Reed, from documents decidedly authentic--so authentic as to have led to their partial destruction, by his vain and silly descendants, who imagined that *truth* could be extinguished, while vanity was kindling a spurious flame to consummate an imaginery *apotheosis*, for one whose actual deeds consigned him to the keeping of the furies and his country's execration.

If such men are to be allowed an enrolment on the page of fame, as revolutionary patriots, who achieved our independence, there is no merits in those who stood side by side with Washington, in the darkest hour of the

Revolution, when dismay sat on the bravest brow--spurning the temptation of British bribes--bidding defiance to British battalions, and enduring the pangs of hunger, thirst, and howling blasts--naked amidst winter's snow, with earth for a pillow, and the canopy of heaven for a covering--treason thundering in their ears--rewards offered for their heads, and nothing but liberty and independence, with the secret assurance of heaven's succour from a just God, to cheer and console them--bleeding, dying, desolate. Shall the *time-serving* traitor take his position by the side of such men? Shall all merit be levelled into one common mass of calculating selfishness? For such must be the effect, if General Joseph Reed is to occupy a niche of glory in the same temple with George Washington. But there is no moral crucible to melt down such deeds into a general and indiscriminate mass. Truth revolts from such profanation. Justice spurns the contamination. Nature herself rises up in arms against the thought, as doing violence to all her holiest sympathies; her purest heart-throbs, her noblest aspirations. God himself denounces the impiety.

Having demonstrated the importance of the revelations of "Valley Forge" to the truth and accuracy of history--of that history, in which we are all so intensely interested--as belonging to the fame of the fathers, and as destined for an inheritance to our children, to the end of time--it remains to consider how the editor of the Evening Journal, in giving publicity to corroborative materials for history, has merited that torrent of scurrility, that has been vomited upon him from the sympathisers in the royal cause of George the Third--who, even up to this day, still retain in their veins, the poison of tory blood! "Valley Forge" makes no *fresh* charge against the tories of 1776. He but deals in specifications of treasonable designs, common to every history of our Revolution, and to be found in every life of George Washington. If he has ventured on the daring task of committing fabrications of letters from General Smith to Colonel ----, he has perpetrated *supererogatory* crime, for no sensible purpose--for all that General Smith's letters told us, we knew before, as notorious facts of history. For this reason, we do not believe he has committed "forgery"--from the mere love of crime, or any other motive. If, then, the sympathisers in the Royal cause, are so offended by these letters, as to pour forth the phials of their wrath upon the editor of this paper, it must be from some other motive than virtuous sensibility or wounded patriotism. But this is not all. What was the character--what the tendency of the letters of "Valley Forge" who has unquestionably committed a deep injury, in maintaining his anonymous character, and failing to redeem "his gage," thrown down with so much defiance to Mr. Spear Smith--what, we say, was the tendency of his letters? It was laudable, noble, exemplary. It was to vindicate Washington, and his co-patriots, from all suspicion of being associated with General Joseph Reed, the secret royalist--the wavering tory--all which he is known to be, on the authority of Cadwalader, as well as Washington himself--from all suspicion of being associated, we say, with Reed as *a friend*--a bosom, and confidental friend. Their direct tendency is, to exalt the patriots of the Revolution, and to depress those English spies in the American uniform, who correspond in cypher, with the royal commissioners, and sought to sell the liberties of their country, for a price, at the very crisis of her fate. And what reply is made to "Valley Forge?" Do the parties criminated, defend their ancestor? No.--Do they question the truth of history? No.--But they charge "Valley Forge," with fabrication. Yet, if he be guilty, does it make Reed innocent? No.--Then why not defend themselves?

VALLEY FORGE.

October, 31st,

We give another communication to-day, from the writer of the articles under this signature. We are satisfied that Valley Forge is what he represents himself to be--that he is sincere, honest, and will, as soon as circumstances will permit, establish the authenticity of every document he has furnished for publication. We shall refrain from pushing our searches any further, for the purpose of discovering the person of Valley Forge, for the good reason that we are satisfied that we know him already. On comparing the note of the 14th inst., to us, written evidently by Valley Forge himself, but in a disguised hand, with a letter of a recent date, in the natural handwriting of the person who we believe assumes that name, there are innumerable evidences that most clearly establish his identity, satisfactorily to us.

A word to our enemies now. Let them go on and pour forth their malice, give full vent to their venom, and pile obloquy, mountain high; we regard it as the idle wind, that passeth by and harmeth not. We have long been accustomed to be traduced and slandered. For making the exposition of the mal-appropriation of the money of the Bank of the United States, by Mr. Biddle, the first that was ever made, we brought down on our head the whole weight of the power of that institution and its legions of friends and supporters. We were charged with having perjured ourselves in that matter. And what has become of that charge now? No one believes it. We have triumphed over all the allegations made against us in the matter, and thousands of individuals are left to weep now, because they did not believe, and act on our testimony at the time it was given.

So in the present case, we are charged with publishing forged letters, and even with forging them ourselves. But on what authority? Why, on the assertion of Mr. John Spear Smith, of Baltimore, made, we do not doubt, in all sincerity, but evidently hastily, and without giving a single reason for his coming to that conclusion.

We do not entertain a single apprehenson but that in this case, every thing will very soon come out right, and that we shall triumph over our enemies and their slanders, as we did in the affair of the Bank of the United States. ***Nous Verrons.***

NOTES:

[A] Reed always said that this reply was the joint protection of Benj.
Rush, Dr Wm. Smith and Gen. John Cadwalader.

[B] See Gov. Johnstone's speech in the House of Commons, March, 9th, 1779,
to be found in the Philadelphia Library in a volume of the Pennsylvania
Packet, February 20th, 1779, No. 384.

[C] Mrs. Ferguson's letter will be found in the same volume in the Numbers
for February 20th, and March 9th.

[D] Here the following anecdote will afford an occasion of recriminating.
When Mr. Reed was proposed as a Brigadier in the army, Mr. John Adams, now
our minister in Holland, openly objected, in Congress, to his appointment,
saying he was of a factious spirit, and had been notoriously instrumental
in fomenting discords between the troops of the different States.

[E] When Mr. Ingersoll waited on me with General Reed's first letter, 9th
of September last, I mentioned to him the situation of my family, and the
necessity of my leaving the city. This has been candidly related by Mr.
Ingersoll to Mr. Reed, as appears by the following extract from his letter,
in answer to mine on the 17th of March, on this subject.

Extract from Mr. Ingersoll's letter, dated Philadelphia, 8th March, 1783.

> "The conversation that passed, I reported with candour, and I
> believe with precision, but still supposed, that the reply
> from General Reed would be founded entirely upon your answer.
> Your declaration, with respect to your intention of leaving
> town, I think I can repeat in nearly the words in which you
> expressed yourself.

"After discoursing upon the subject of the letter I had put
into your hands, you mentioned to me that your furniture was
packed up to go to Maryland; that you had been waiting for
rain to lay the dust, and that if anything was to come of this
business, it must be *speedily*.

"I ENDEAVOUR to give the *words* used,--I certainly do not
deviate from the *purport* of what was said."

This is not the least of the many *misrepresentations* in
which Mr. Reed is convicted in the course of my reply.

[F] Being called upon by General Cadwalader to recollect the conversation
we had at the Coffee-House, in the fall of the year seventy-eight, when he
related what had passed between him and Mr. Reed at Bristol, I remember the
subject corroborates with those queries I have since seen published in Mr.
Oswald's paper, of the 7th of September, 1782. I likewise remember giving
him a hint, that some of Mr. Reed's friends were present, on which he
repeated what he had related before, and then addressed himself to the
gentlemen, and informed them, if any of Mr. Reed's friends were present,
they were at liberty to make what use they pleased of it.

THOMAS PRYOR.

Philadelphia, March 8, 1783.

[G] See Gen. Reed's Address to the Public, pages 24, 25.

[H] As a proof of my having made this declaration, and the occasion of it,
I offer the following letter:

DEAR SIR:--I have, at your request, charged my recollection with what fell from you, in the hearing of myself and several others, at the trial of Mr. William Hamilton, on the subject of Mr. Reed, who assisted the prosecution; it was in terms to this effect; that it indicated the extremity of baseness in him, to attempt to destroy another for taking the very step he had once lifted his own foot to take. This, at the instant, made a deeper impression me, as having never till then, though living in the closest intimacy, heard you drop the most distant hint of any intended defection of Mr. Reed, of which I myself had no suspicion.

    Your humble servant,
    GEORGE CLYMER.
March 2d, 1783.
General Cadwalader.

[I] If the countryman was sent, as he insinuated, for intelligence, and not for a protection for Mr. Reed and his friend, is it not very extraordinary, in a case of this nature, after the man had so narrowly escaped with his life, that no circumstance relating to so delicate an affair, (transacted in so private a manner) should ever have come to my knowledge, till I heard this testimony from Major Lennox?

I will venture to say that no officer of the army, at that critical period, would have risked his reputation, though he had afforded no cause to suspect his firmness, by instructing a spy to apply for a protection for him, with a view of gaining intelligence, without mentioning it to his commanding officer before the transaction. But in the instance before us, it is worthy notice, that in so critical a situation of public affairs, Mr. Reed, knowing how dangerous such a plea as the messenger had used might prove to his reputation, in the hands of the enemy, should not have endeavoured to obviate such a tale, by mentioning the circumstance to the commanding officer at Bristol, who might have vouched for his innocence, in case Donop should attempt to injure him afterwards.

[J] I have ample proofs of Mr. Ellis's attachment to the enemy, which may be produced, if necessary.

[K]

M'Kenney's Ferry, 25th December, 1776, 6 o'clock, P. M.

Dear Sir,--Notwithstanding the discouraging accounts I have received from Col. Reed, of what might be expected from the operations below, I am determined, as the night is favourable, to cross the river, and make the attack on Trenton in the morning. If you can do nothing real, at least create as great a diversion as possible.

I am, sir, your most obedient servant,

GEO. WASHINGTON.

[L] The following extracts from General Reed's letter to his Excellency the President and the Honorable the Executive Council of the State of Pennsylvania, dated Philadelphia, 22d July, 1777, assigning his reasons for not accepting the office of Chief Justice, may serve to prove his opinions of the constitution at that time. "If there is any radical weakness of authority proceeding from the Constitution; if in any respects it opposes the genius, temper or habits of the governed, *I fear, unless a remedy can be provided, in less than seven years, government will sink in a spiritless langour, or expire in a sudden* CONVULSION. It would be foreign to my present purpose to suggest any of those *alterations*, which, in my *apprehension are necessary* to enable the constitution to support itself with *dignity* and *efficiency*, and its friends with *security. That some are necessary I cannot entertain the least doubt.* With this sentiment, I feel an *insuperable difficulty* to enter into an engagement of the *most solemn nature*, leading to the *support* and *confirmation* of an entire system of government, which I cannot wholly **approve**." Again, "the dispensation from this engagement,[M] first allowed to several members of the Assembly, and afterwards to the militia officers, has added to my **difficulties**, as I cannot reconcile it to my ideas of propriety, the members of the same state being under different obligations to support and enforce its authority." But he adds, "If the sense of the people who have the right of decision, leads to some alterations, I firmly believe it will conduce to our happiness and security; if otherwise, I shall esteem it my duty, not only to acquiesce, but to support as far as lays in my power, a form of government confirmed and sanctified by the voice of the people." Here, then, he says, "he feels an **insuperable difficulty** to enter into an engagement of the most solemn nature, leading to the support and confirmation of an entire system of government, which he cannot wholly **approve**; but he shall think it his duty to acquiesce, and support the government,--if confirmed and sanctified by the voice of the people." How inconsistent, then, must his conduct appear, when it is notorious, that he took a decided part in support of government, accepted of his seat in Council, and afterwards the Presidency, long before the sense of the people was expressd by the **fabricated instructions** to the members of Assembly, requiring them to rescind the resolution for calling a convention for the purpose of revising the constitution. And yet he says, in the 27th page of his pamphlet, he "so effectually vindicated every part of his conduct, that every gentleman present, (myself excepted,) acknowledged his mistake."

These were the ostensible reasons for not accepting the Chief Justiceship, and taking the oath of office; but an oath of another kind, no doubt, induced him to decline this appointment. He had not taken the oath of allegiance which the law, (passed the 13th June, 1777,) required of every male white inhabitant; nor did he take it, as appears by the publication signed Sidney, in the Pennsylvania Journal, No. 1565, 12th February, 1783,) till the 9th of October, 1778, which was the very day he was elected a Councillor for the County of Philadelphia. And though disfranchised of all the rights of citizenship, and incapable of being elected into, or serving in any office, place, or trust, in this commonwealth, Mr. Reed dared to disregard the voice of the people, and violate the law, by accepting the Presidency, and exercising the powers of government annexed to that office. If he had taken the oath of allegiance, agreeable to law, why did he take it ***again***, on the day he was elected a councillor? as the mere oath of office only, upon that occasion, would have been required of him.

As Mr. Reed has not touched this point in his pamphlet, or furnished his friends with a single argument to defend him, against a charge supported by authentic proofs from public records, the public have very justly pronounced him guilty. If certificates can be produced of his oaths of abjuration and allegiance, agreeable to law, why have they not been published? If he is not defranchised of the rights of citizenship, why was his vote refused at the last election? or is this one of the subjects reserved for "***legal examination***?" and if so, why does he not suspend the public opinion by such information?

[M] *By the "dispensation from this engagement," above mentioned, is meant,*
that the oath prescribed by the constitution was dispensed with, and many members of Assembly were permitted to take another oath, in which they were
not bound to support the constitution.

[N] That this opinion was not entertained by Congress, may reasonably be inferred from the following letter:

"*Philadelphia, 12th September, 1778.*

"SIR,--His excellency, General Washington, having recommended to Congress the appointment of a General of horse, the House took that subject under consideration the 10th instant, when you were unanimously elected Brigadier and commander of the cavalry in the service of the United States.

"From the general view above mentioned, you will perceive, sir, the earnest desire of the house, that you will accept a commission, and enter as early as your convenience will admit of, upon the duties of the office; and I flatter myself with hopes of congratulating you in a few days upon this occasion.

"I have the honour to be, with particular regard and esteem, sir, your most humble servant,

HENRY LAURENS,
 "The Hon. Brigadier-General Cadwalader.   "President of Congress,"

But not wishing to have it suggested, that I entered into the service at so late a period of the war for the sake of rank, as the French treaty had taken place, and I had conceived all offensive operations at an end, I declined the appointment in these terms.

Maryland, 19th September, 1778.

SIR,--I have the highest sense of the honour conferred upon me by Congress, in appointing me a Brigadier in the Continental service, with the command of the cavalry, more particularly as the voice of Congress was unanimous.

I cannot consent to enter into the service at this time, as the war appears to me to be near the close. But should any misfortune give an unhappy turn to our affairs, I shall immediately apply to Congress for a command in the army.

I have the honour to be, with the greatest regard and esteem, your excellency's most obedient humble servant,

JOHN CADWALADER.

His Excellency Henry Laurens, Esq.,   President of Congress.

www.bookjungle.com *email: sales@bookjungle.com fax: 630-214-0564 mail: Book Jungle PO Box 2226 Champaign, IL 61825*

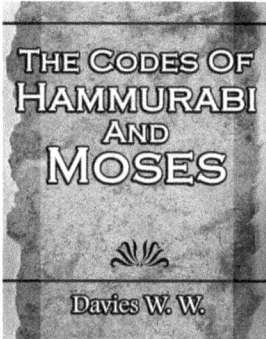

The Codes Of Hammurabi And Moses
W. W. Davies

QTY

The discovery of the Hammurabi Code is one of the greatest achievements of archaeology, and is of paramount interest, not only to the student of the Bible, but also to all those interested in ancient history...

Religion   **ISBN:** *1-59462-338-4*   **Pages:132**
MSRP $12.95

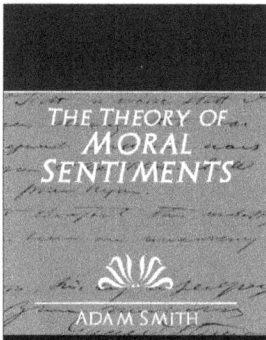

The Theory of Moral Sentiments
Adam Smith

QTY

This work from 1749. contains original theories of conscience amd moral judgment and it is the foundation for systemof morals.

Philosophy **ISBN:** *1-59462-777-0*   **Pages:536**
MSRP $19.95

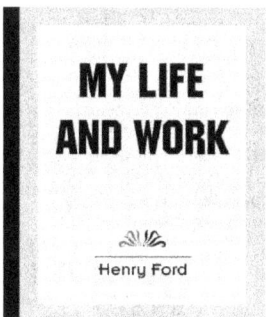

Jessica's First Prayer
Hesba Stretton

QTY

In a screened and secluded corner of one of the many railway-bridges which span the streets of London there could be seen a few years ago, from five o'clock every morning until half past eight, a tidily set-out coffee-stall, consisting of a trestle and board, upon which stood two large tin cans, with a small fire of charcoal burning under each so as to keep the coffee boiling during the early hours of the morning when the work-people were thronging into the city on their way to their daily toil...

Pages:84

Childrens   **ISBN:** *1-59462-373-2*   *MSRP $9.95*

My Life and Work
Henry Ford

QTY

Henry Ford revolutionized the world with his implementation of mass production for the Model T automobile. Gain valuable business insight into his life and work with his own auto-biography... "We have only started on our development of our country we have not as yet, with all our talk of wonderful progress, done more than scratch the surface. The progress has been wonderful enough but..."

Pages:300

Biographies/   **ISBN:** *1-59462-198-5*   *MSRP $21.95*

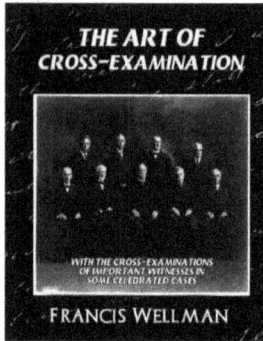

The Art of Cross-Examination
Francis Wellman

QTY

I presume it is the experience of every author, after his first book is published upon an important subject, to be almost overwhelmed with a wealth of ideas and illustrations which could readily have been included in his book, and which to his own mind, at least, seem to make a second edition inevitable. Such certainly was the case with me; and when the first edition had reached its sixth impression in five months, I rejoiced to learn that it seemed to my publishers that the book had met with a sufficiently favorable reception to justify a second and considerably enlarged edition. ..

Pages:412

Reference   ISBN: *1-59462-647-2*   *MSRP $19.95*

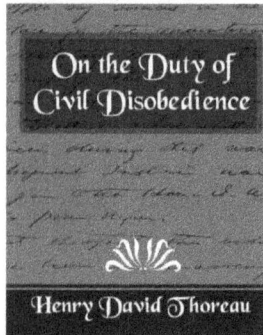

On the Duty of Civil Disobedience
Henry David Thoreau

QTY

Thoreau wrote his famous essay, On the Duty of Civil Disobedience, as a protest against an unjust but popular war and the immoral but popular institution of slave-owning. He did more than write—he declined to pay his taxes, and was hauled off to gaol in consequence. Who can say how much this refusal of his hastened the end of the war and of slavery ?

Law   ISBN: *1-59462-747-9*   **Pages:48**
                                          MSRP $7.45

Dream Psychology Psychoanalysis for Beginners
Sigmund Freud

QTY

Sigmund Freud, born Sigismund Schlomo Freud (May 6, 1856 - September 23, 1939), was a Jewish-Austrian neurologist and psychiatrist who co-founded the psychoanalytic school of psychology. Freud is best known for his theories of the unconscious mind, especially involving the mechanism of repression; his redefinition of sexual desire as mobile and directed towards a wide variety of objects; and his therapeutic techniques, especially his understanding of transference in the therapeutic relationship and the presumed value of dreams as sources of insight into unconscious desires.

Pages:196

Psychology   ISBN: *1-59462-905-6*   *MSRP $15.45*

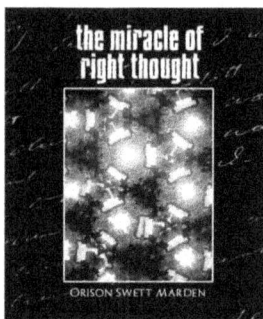

The Miracle of Right Thought
Orison Swett Marden

QTY

Believe with all of your heart that you will do what you were made to do. When the mind has once formed the habit of holding cheerful, happy, prosperous pictures, it will not be easy to form the opposite habit. It does not matter how improbable or how far away this realization may see, or how dark the prospects may be, if we visualize them as best we can, as vividly as possible, hold tenaciously to them and vigorously struggle to attain them, they will gradually become actualized, realized in the life. But a desire, a longing without endeavor, a yearning abandoned or held indifferently will vanish without realization.

Pages:360

Self Help   ISBN: *1-59462-644-8*   *MSRP $25.45*

The Rosicrucian Cosmo-Conception Mystic Christianity by *Max Heindel* ISBN: *1-59462-188-8* **$38.95**
The Rosicrucian Cosmo-conception is not dogmatic, neither does it appeal to any other authority than the reason of the student. It is: not controversial, but is: sent forth in the, hope that it may help to clear... New Age/Religion Pages 646

Abandonment To Divine Providence by *Jean-Pierre de Caussade* ISBN: *1-59462-228-0* **$25.95**
"The Rev. Jean Pierre de Caussade was one of the most remarkable spiritual writers of the Society of Jesus in France in the 18th Century. His death took place at Toulouse in 1751. His works have gone through many editions and have been republished... Inspirational/Religion Pages 400

Mental Chemistry by *Charles Haanel* ISBN: *1-59462-192-6* **$23.95**
Mental Chemistry allows the change of material conditions by combining and appropriately utilizing the power of the mind. Much like applied chemistry creates something new and unique out of careful combinations of chemicals the mastery of mental chemistry... New Age Pages 354

The Letters of Robert Browning and Elizabeth Barret Barrett 1845-1846 vol II ISBN: *1-59462-193-4* **$35.95**
by *Robert Browning* and *Elizabeth Barrett* Biographies Pages 596

Gleanings In Genesis (volume I) by *Arthur W. Pink* ISBN: *1-59462-130-6* **$27.45**
Appropriately has Genesis been termed "the seed plot of the Bible" for in it we have, in germ form, almost all of the great doctrines which are afterwards fully developed in the books of Scripture which follow... Religion/Inspirational Pages 420

The Master Key by *L. W. de Laurence* ISBN: *1-59462-001-6* **$30.95**
In no branch of human knowledge has there been a more lively increase of the spirit of research during the past few years than in the study of Psychology, Concentration and Mental Discipline. The requests for authentic lessons in Thought Control, Mental Discipline and... New Age/Business Pages 422

The Lesser Key Of Solomon Goetia by *L. W. de Laurence* ISBN: *1-59462-092-X* **$9.95**
This translation of the first book of the "Lemegton" which is now for the first time made accessible to students of Talismanic Magic was done, after careful collation and edition, from numerous Ancient Manuscripts in Hebrew, Latin, and French... New Age/Occult Pages 92

Rubaiyat Of Omar Khayyam by *Edward Fitzgerald* ISBN:*1-59462-332-5* **$13.95**
Edward Fitzgerald, whom the world has already learned, in spite of his own efforts to remain within the shadow of anonymity, to look upon as one of the rarest poets of the century, was born at Bredfield, in Suffolk, on the 31st of March, 1809. He was the third son of John Purcell... Music Pages 172

Ancient Law by *Henry Maine* ISBN: *1-59462-128-4* **$29.95**
The chief object of the following pages is to indicate some of the earliest ideas of mankind, as they are reflected in Ancient Law, and to point out the relation of those ideas to modern thought. Religion/History Pages 452

Far-Away Stories by *William J. Locke* ISBN: *1-59462-129-2* **$19.45**
"Good wine needs no bush, but a collection of mixed vintages does. And this book is just such a collection. Some of the stories I do not want to remain buried for ever in the museum files of dead magazine-numbers an author's not unpardonable vanity..." Fiction Pages 272

Life of David Crockett by *David Crockett* ISBN: *1-59462-250-7* **$27.45**
"Colonel David Crockett was one of the most remarkable men of the times in which he lived. Born in humble life, but gifted with a strong will, an indomitable courage, and unremitting perseverance... Biographies/New Age Pages 424

Lip-Reading by *Edward Nitchie* ISBN: *1-59462-206-X* **$25.95**
Edward B. Nitchie, founder of the New York School for the Hard of Hearing, now the Nitchie School of Lip-Reading, Inc, wrote "LIP-READING Principles and Practice". The development and perfecting of this meritorious work on lip-reading was an undertaking... How-to Pages 400

A Handbook of Suggestive Therapeutics, Applied Hypnotism, Psychic Science ISBN: *1-59462-214-0* **$24.95**
by *Henry Munro* Health/New Age/Health/Self-help Pages 376

A Doll's House: and Two Other Plays by *Henrik Ibsen* ISBN: *1-59462-112-8* **$19.95**
Henrik Ibsen created this classic when in revolutionary 1848 Rome. Introducing some striking concepts in playwriting for the realist genre, this play has been studied the world over. Fiction/Classics/Plays 308

The Light of Asia by *sir Edwin Arnold* ISBN: *1-59462-204-3* **$13.95**
In this poetic masterpiece, Edwin Arnold describes the life and teachings of Buddha. The man who was to become known as Buddha to the world was born as Prince Gautama of India but he rejected the worldly riches and abandoned the reigns of power when... Religion/History/Biographies Pages 170

The Complete Works of Guy de Maupassant by *Guy de Maupassant* ISBN: *1-59462-157-8* **$16.95**
"For days and days, nights and nights, I had dreamed of that first kiss which was to consecrate our engagement, and I knew not on what spot I should put my lips..." Fiction/Classics Pages 240

The Art of Cross-Examination by *Francis L. Wellman* ISBN: *1-59462-309-0* **$26.95**
Written by a renowned trial lawyer, Wellman imparts his experience and uses case studies to explain how to use psychology to extract desired information through questioning. How-to/Science/Reference Pages 408

Answered or Unanswered? by *Louisa Vaughan* ISBN: *1-59462-248-5* **$10.95**
Miracles of Faith in China Religion Pages 112

The Edinburgh Lectures on Mental Science (1909) by *Thomas* ISBN: *1-59462-008-3* **$11.95**
This book contains the substance of a course of lectures recently given by the writer in the Queen Street Hall, Edinburgh. Its purpose is to indicate the Natural Principles governing the relation between Mental Action and Material Conditions... New Age/Psychology Pages 148

Ayesha by *H. Rider Haggard* ISBN: *1-59462-301-5* **$24.95**
Verily and indeed it is the unexpected that happens! Probably if there was one person upon the earth from whom the Editor of this, and of a certain previous history, did not expect to hear again... Classics Pages 380

Ayala's Angel by *Anthony Trollope* ISBN: *1-59462-352-X* **$29.95**
The two girls were both pretty, but Lucy who was twenty-one who supposed to be simple and comparatively unattractive, whereas Ayala was credited, as her Bombwhat romantic name might show, with poetic charm and a taste for romance. Ayala when her father died was nineteen... Fiction Pages 484

The American Commonwealth by *James Bryce* ISBN: *1-59462-286-8* **$34.45**
An interpretation of American democratic political theory. It examines political mechanics and society from the perspective of Scotsman James Bryce Politics Pages 572

Stories of the Pilgrims by *Margaret P. Pumphrey* ISBN: *1-59462-116-0* **$17.95**
This book explores pilgrims religious oppression in England as well as their escape to Holland and eventual crossing to America on the Mayflower, and their early days in New England... History Pages 268

www.bookjungle.com *email: sales@bookjungle.com fax: 630-214-0564 mail: Book Jungle PO Box 2226 Champaign, IL 61825*

QTY

The Fasting Cure *by Sinclair Upton*   ISBN: *1-59462-222-1*   **$13.95**
In the Cosmopolitan Magazine for May, 1910, and in the Contemporary Review (London) for April, 1910, I published an article dealing with my experiences in fasting. I have written a great many magazine articles, but never one which attracted so much attention... New Age/Self Help/Health Pages 164

Hebrew Astrology *by Sepharial*   ISBN: *1-59462-308-2*   **$13.45**
In these days of advanced thinking it is a matter of common observation that we have left many of the old landmarks behind and that we are now pressing forward to greater heights and to a wider horizon than that which represented the mind-content of our progenitors...   Astrology Pages 144

Thought Vibration or The Law of Attraction in the Thought World   ISBN: *1-59462-127-6*   **$12.95**
by William Walker Atkinson   *Psychology/Religion Pages 144*

Optimism *by Helen Keller*   ISBN: *1-59462-108-X*   **$15.95**
Helen Keller was blind, deaf, and mute since 19 months old, yet famously learned how to overcome these handicaps, communicate with the world, and spread her lectures promoting optimism. An inspiring read for everyone...   Biographies/Inspirational Pages 84

Sara Crewe *by Frances Burnett*   ISBN: *1-59462-360-0*   **$9.45**
In the first place, Miss Minchin lived in London. Her home was a large, dull, tall one, in a large, dull square, where all the houses were alike, and all the sparrows were alike, and where all the door-knockers made the same heavy sound...   Childrens/Classic Pages 88

The Autobiography of Benjamin Franklin *by Benjamin Franklin*   ISBN: *1-59462-135-7*   **$24.95**
The Autobiography of Benjamin Franklin has probably been more extensively read than any other American historical work, and no other book of its kind has had such ups and downs of fortune. Franklin lived for many years in England, where he was agent...   Biographies/History Pages 332

Name	
Email	
Telephone	
Address	
City, State ZIP	

☐ **Credit Card**   ☐ **Check / Money Order**

Credit Card Number	
Expiration Date	
Signature	

Please Mail to: Book Jungle
PO Box 2226
Champaign, IL 61825
or Fax to: 630-214-0564

ORDERING INFORMATION

web: *www.bookjungle.com*
email: *sales@bookjungle.com*
fax: *630-214-0564*
mail: *Book Jungle PO Box 2226 Champaign, IL 61825*
or PayPal *to sales@bookjungle.com*

Please contact us for bulk discounts

DIRECT-ORDER TERMS

**20% Discount if You Order
Two or More Books**
Free Domestic Shipping!
Accepted: Master Card, Visa,
Discover, American Express

www.ingramcontent.com/pod-product-compliance
Lightning Source LLC
Chambersburg PA
CBHW081233090426

42738CB00016B/3287